Words of Lif

Frances Hogan i[...]
is working as a lay missionary [...]
taught Science and Scripture in West Africa and
Ireland for nine years. Since 1975 she has worked full-
time as a lay missionary, giving scripture courses,
retreats, and working in parishes opening up the
scriptures to the people.

Frances Hogan has committed her life to making
the Word of God known to lay people in the Church
in order to deepen their prayer life and commitment
to Christ. She has made a series of *Scripture Tapes*
on books of the Bible and on various spiritual
themes.

Frances Hogan

Words of Life

Foreword by
Bishop Langton D. Fox,
Retired Bishop of Menevia, Wales

Collins
FOUNT PAPERBACKS

First published in Great Britain in 1984
by Fount Paperbacks, London

Made and printed in Great Britain by
William Collins Sons & Co. Ltd, Glasgow

For my Father, to whom, under God, I owe the gift of life, and whatever love of God and Scripture I possess. With grateful thanks.

Contents

Foreword

Frances Hogan is a smiling, serene Dubliner with a special gift for teaching. She has charmed thousands of us with her talks on Scripture.

She is a clear-minded, centre-of-the-road, Vatican II Catholic, and her gift is for presenting the whole of Sacred Scripture, not only the New Testament, to twentieth-century Catholics. When she presents them, the books that make up the Bible cause 'our hearts to burn within us' (Luke 24:32). They reveal their quality as letters from heaven sent with love by our Father who wants us to know Him and follow His guidance.

Helpfully, Frances has made sound-tapes of her talks available. Now she offers this book in which she talks to us of Exodus. I say 'she talks to us' because her style is that of the spoken word. She gives a sense of direct personal communication. She makes easy reading.

She is informative, but mercifully she is economic about the wealth of information she could pass on. The load of evidence about authorship, for example, or about the documents woven into the text, even verse-by-verse commentary, we can find elsewhere. Frances gives us only what we need that we may clearly understand and warmly receive what God tells us through Exodus of how He wants us to respond to His leadership (2 Timothy 3:16) and what, in His love, He wants us to know about Himself.

You study the scriptures
believing that in them you have eternal life;
now these same scriptures testify to me (John 5:39).

†Langton D. Fox   Retired Bishop of Menevia, Wales

Introduction

The Old Testament is a treasury of God's Word to us, containing rich spiritual nourishment. Some people think that it has nothing relevant to say to them. They read it with little understanding, then put it aside as being for scholars. But St Paul tells us that 'all Scripture is inspired by God and can profitably be used for teaching, for refuting error, for guiding people's lives and for teaching them to be holy' (2 Timothy 3:16). The Book of Exodus can help our spiritual growth, even though the events that it chronicles took place over three thousand years ago. God chose to reveal Himself through the people of Israel and through their history, and He spoke through them a universal message to mankind. This message of redemption forms the central theme of the Book of Exodus.

The Book of Exodus is the most important book of the Old Testament; without it Israel's history in particular, and the Bible in general, would be unintelligible. The Bible opens with the Book of Genesis, which describes the creation and fall of mankind, and our desperate need of a saviour. Exodus follows as the second book of the Pentateuch (which means 'five rolls'), the most important section of the Old Testament. The other three books of the Pentateuch comprise Leviticus (The Book of Holiness), Numbers (The Wilderness Book), and Deuteronomy (The Renewal of the Law). The title of this second book comes from the Greek 'Exodos' which means 'the exit' or 'the way out'. The Hebrew title was *Shemoth*, 'these are the Names', but it is no longer used.

It is not my intention to give you a verse-by-verse commentary on the Book of Exodus, but rather to show you the pattern of redemption, and to indicate some of its many lessons for daily life.

The plan of redemption was first revealed by God in a partial way through signs and symbols in the exodus of Israel from Egypt: the completion and fulfilment came through Christ and the gospels. This partial revelation is known as a shadow or a type. The main theme of the gospels is that Jesus, the Son of God, became incarnate 'to seek out and save that which was lost' (Luke 19:10), to make His people into children of God and form them into a worshipping community, the Church, through His death and Resurrection. The main theme of the Old Testament is that Yahweh had compassion on a group of slaves in Egypt and came down to deliver them through Moses, His chosen redeemer (Exodus 3:7–8), made them into the people of God and formed them through the Covenant into a worshipping community. The Church-nation of Israel gave way to the Church proper in the New Testament.

Jesus Himself guided the young Church to go back to the Old Testament to interpret the redemption wrought by the Messiah: 'then starting with Moses and going through all the prophets he explained to them the passages throughout the scriptures that were about himself' (Luke 24:27; see also v. 44). This typological interpretation is used extensively throughout the New Testament (cf. 1 Corinthians 10:1–13; 2 Corinthians 3:6–18; Romans 4:23, 5:14, etc.; all of the Letter to the Hebrews), among the early church Fathers, and is the interpretation used in this book. It means that we go beyond the record of historical events to find out what God wanted to teach us through them. We go beyond the question 'Did it happen?' (history) to 'What does it mean?', 'What is God saying to us?' (revelation), and meet the living and powerful Word of God.

From this viewpoint we see in Moses a figure foreshadowing Christ, in Pharaoh a type of devil, and in Egypt the world without God, while the Hebrew slaves point to all those who are in need of redemption. The

12

purpose of redemption is God's desire to bring His people out of slavery and into intimacy with Himself. Our slavery to sin is seen typified in the physical slavery of the Hebrews. God sent them a saviour – Moses in the Old Testament, and Jesus in the New, who made God known to the people and revealed His Word to them (Exodus 3 onwards, cf. John 17 '. . . and I have made your Name known to them . . .'). But the people will not believe 'unless they see signs and wonders' (John 4:48), so God manifested His signs through the plagues of Moses and the miracles of Jesus; both suffered conflicts with the authorities – in Pharaoh (Old Testament) and the leaders of Israel (New Testament). Redemption was brought about by blood sacrifice, in the death of the Passover Lamb (Old Testament) and Jesus on Calvary (New Testament). For neither Hebrews nor Christians was this the end of the story, for their pilgrim journey had only begun when slavery and death were overcome in that Easter garden which had been foreshadowed by the Passover. The exodus or 'going out' of God's people began when Moses led them into their baptism in the Red Sea (cf. 1 Corinthians 10:1–4), through the wilderness where they were tried and tested, to their meeting with God at Sinai. There God manifested His glory to them and bound them to Himself by the solemn covenant which obliged them to love and serve God and their neighbour (cf. Exodus 20; John 13:34). They became God's Church-nation just as Jesus formed the universal Church whose sign is obedience to God's will and love for God and neighbour as the expression of the New Covenant in His own blood. The Church-nation was commissioned to conquer the Promised Land and set up the Kingdom of God, but they failed and this is now the mandate of the Church.

The early church Fathers looked for the deep mystical meaning of the scriptures to feed their people. Here are a few examples from their works. St Basil says:

> . . . the faith in Moses and in the cloud is as it were, in

a shadow and type . . . The type is our exhibition of the things expected and gives an imitative anticipation of the future . . . typically 'that rock was Christ'; and the water a type of the living power of the word, as it says 'if any man is thirsty let him come to me and drink'. The manna is a type of the living bread that came down from heaven . . . so in like manner the history of the exodus of Israel is recorded to show forth those who are being saved through baptism. For the firstborn of the Israelites were preserved, like the bodies of the baptized, by the giving of Grace to them that were marked with blood. For the blood of the sheep is a type of the blood of Christ . . . the sea is typically a baptism bringing about the departure from Pharaoh, in like manner as this washing (baptism) causes the departure of the tyranny of the devil. The sea slew the enemy in itself and in baptism too dies our enemy towards God. From the sea the people came out unharmed: we too, as it were, alive from the dead, step up from the water 'saved' by the 'grace' of Him who called us. (Second series, Volume 8, chapter 14, No. 31)

That great biblical scholar, St Jerome, wrote that:

as wood sweetens Marah so that seventy palm trees were watered by its streams, so the cross makes the waters of the Law life-giving for the seventy who are Christ's Apostles. (Letter LXIX, No. 6)

St Ambrose made this comparison:

He cast down the rod and it became a serpent which devoured the serpents of Egypt thus signifying that the word should become flesh to destroy the poison of the dread serpent by the forgiveness and pardon of sins. For the rod stands for the Word that is true, royal, filled with power, glorious in ruling . . . (Duties of clergy, Book III, chapter 15, No. 94. Citations from *The Nicene and Post-*

Introduction

Nicene Fathers of the Christian Church, edited by Philip Schaff; published by Wm. B. Eerdmans Publishing Co., Grand Rapids, 1956)

It is universally accepted that Moses is the main author of the Book of Exodus – both its narrative and legislative sections. God instructed Moses to write everything down for future generations (cf. Exodus 17:14, 24:4, 34:27; Numbers 33:2; Deuteronomy 31:9,24; Matthew 19:8; Mark 12:26; Luke 24:44; John 5:45–47). Like every other book in the Bible, this original corpus went through many changes and developments with time, so that the Mosaic material became the nucleus of what we now call the Pentateuch, which although it covers the first five books of the Bible is one single unified historical and theological work.

Four strands or traditions are easily identified as the main sources of this work. They are the Yahwistic, Elohistic, Deuteronomistic and Priestly sources – usually referred to as the JEDP documents. They represent different schools of thought; they interpret the events of God's intervention in human history from different viewpoints. Over the centuries these sources were fused into one text and reworked by editors to give the final form of the book as we find it in our Bibles.

As each source was considered sacred, the final editors did not remove duplications of material from the text (cf. Exodus 3:1–20 and 6:2–13, 6:28–7:7, chapters 25–31 and 35–39). Our Book of Exodus represents the last edition of this work, and is accepted by Jews and Christians as inspired by God. We see therefore that God used not only Moses, but many people whose identity is unknown to us, to produce this work.

The oldest documentary source comes from the tenth century BC – probably during the reign of King Solomon. It deals with the narrative section of the national saga, and as its authors used 'Yahweh' for the divine name it is called the Yahwist document or the 'J' document. After Israel was divided into two kingdoms the account of God's wonderful dealings with his people began to be handed down in different versions in both kingdoms. By the eighth century BC the 'E' document had appeared – so called because its authors' preferred ELOHIM for the divine name. At a later stage, when the northern kingdom had been destroyed, these two documents were fused into one – the 'JE' text – while at the same time the priests of the northern kingdom were producing the third source – known as the 'D' document, as it is mostly found in the Book of Deuteronomy. Since the priests were mainly interested in legal codes, liturgy and worship in the Temple, their document is easily identified in the text. The 'P' or priestly document was the last one to be put into writing. It came from the priests in Jerusalem, and is generally held to be based on very ancient sources, but it reached its final stage in the sixth century BC. Somewhere between the sixth century and fifth century BC the final editor (or editors) fused the sources together to give us the final JEDP text. Our present Book of Exodus represents, therefore, a Mosaic nucleus with centuries of reworking of the text and reinterpretation of the events narrated.

We see, then, that scripture has both human and divine authorship since the Holy Spirit is the divine inspirer of the text. Like Jesus, the Word made flesh, it has a human and a divine source, and it is when we accept both of these sources that we appreciate the wonder of its development and of God's provision for us.

Since the historical events which make up the facts related in the Book of Exodus are of such ancient origin, I follow the generally accepted theories whenever there is difficulty. I have used either 'God' or 'the Lord' for the divine name – Yahweh – in the text, even when I quote from the Jerusalem Bible.

Bibliography

Gleanings in Exodus by A. A. Pink; Moody Press, Chicago 1976

When God Formed a People by Michael Maher; Koinonia Press, Manchester 1978

His Way Out by Bernard L. Ramm; G/L Publications, Glendale, California, USA

Number in Scripture by E. W. Bullinger, D.D.; Kregal Publications, Grand Rapids, Michigan. First published 1894, last reprinting 1978

Ancient Israel by Roland de Vaux, O.P.; Darton, Longman & Todd, London 1968

The Companion Bible published by Samuel Bagster & Sons Ltd., London 1974

The Jerome Biblical Commentary, published by Geoffrey Chapman, London 1970

A New Catholic Commentary on Holy Scripture, published by Nelson, 1969

Matthew Henry's Commentary on the Whole Bible, published by Marshall, Morgan & Scott, London 1960

The Men and the Message of the Old Testament by Peter F. Ellis; Liturgical Press, Collegeville, Minnesota 1962

Dictionary of Biblical Theology by Xavier Leon-Dufour; Geoffrey Chapman, London 1978

I. The Time of Bondage

1. Slaves in Egypt

Exodus opens by telling us about the extended family of Jacob, seventy of them, who migrated from the land of Canaan into Egypt because of famine. The fact that they were welcomed in Egypt was because their brother Joseph (whom they had sold as a slave into Egypt many years before) was the ruler of the country under Pharaoh. They were allowed to settle in the Nile delta, the land of Goshen, the most fertile part of Egypt. And because of their relationship to Joseph they were treated as a privileged group. They were shepherds and had large flocks of cattle and sheep.

A very good beginning to a saga that was to end so sadly. For the time being they bought property and settled down in Egypt as if God had called them to live *there*. But it was the land of Canaan that God had promised to Abraham, Isaac, Jacob and their descendants – not Egypt. It seems a strange twist of divine providence that they should settle in Egypt: in fact their stay there was 430 years altogether. That this was a definite part of the divine plan we can see from Genesis. God had told Abraham that his descendants would be exiles in a strange land, where they would be slaves and oppressed for four hundred years. Then He said, 'I will bring judgement on the nation that enslaves them, and after that they will leave with many possessions . . . In the fourth generation they will come back here, for the wickedness of the Amorites is not yet ended' (Genesis 15:13–16).

So what could be the reason for their prolonged stay in Egypt? First, they went into Egypt as a large family, but they were to come out of it a nation. They were given four hundred years to establish themselves: 'Do not be afraid of going down to Egypt, for I will make you a great nation there. I myself will go down to Egypt. I myself will bring you back again . . .' (Genesis 46:3f). Second, the suffering that they would experience in Egypt would detach them from it, and make it easier for them to migrate to Canaan when deliverance came. We shall see later on that they loved Egypt, in spite of all their sufferings. Man is very attached to territory, and to the kingdoms of this world: he finds it very difficult to believe that God is genuinely offering something better. We struggle to hold on to earthly things that seem so tangible and secure, and only suffering can make us see things in a different perspective. Suffering helps us see beyond the immediate, beyond life to eternity, and enables us to make decisions which otherwise would be almost impossible for our weak human nature.

Then, third, there is that strange statement in Genesis that we find hard to come to terms with nowadays: '. . . for the wickedness of the Amorites is not yet ended' (Genesis 15:16). The author seems to be telling us that the Amorites will not be driven from Canaan until they are so far gone in wickedness that a just God has to intervene. And this intervention appears to be the removal of God's protective hand so that their natural enemies can conquer them. Assessing this from a purely historical or political viewpoint you would not come to the same conclusion! But the Bible is a book of revelation, offering only the spiritual standpoint – and from that angle things do look very different. The scriptures show us that God is impartial to all His people, including Israel. If you look at 2 Kings 24 you will see that when Israel broke God's Covenant seriously and manifested great wickedness, God allowed her enemies to conquer and take her to slavery in Babylon for seventy years. She 'went back to square one', because her saga began with deliverance from slavery.

There could be yet another reason from the time in Egypt, a rather sober reason. The scriptures tell us that you reap what you sow, not only on the natural level but also on the spiritual (Galatians 6:7). For example, if you sow dissension in a community you will scarcely expect to reap great harmony! If you sow an apple tree in your garden you can, in time, expect apples. What I am suggesting is that the sons of Jacob had to reap the results of their own action in selling their brother Joseph into slavery. Now they are themselves in Egypt and reduced to slavery. Very often, it is only the consequences of our actions that reveal to us how sinful they were.

Born into slavery
Exodus 1:1. The Hebrews went into Egypt, which led to slavery, 'with their father Jacob'. This reminds us that the whole human race went into slavery to sin, in our father Adam. In the making of this nation all the children of Jacob were born outside the Promised Land, in slavery – just as all the children of Adam were born outside paradise, in slavery to sin.

Here is the beginning of the great spiritual drama that opens with slavery and oppression. There are echoes of this in the parable of the good Samaritan: the road from Jerusalem to Jericho is a symbol of life, with Jerusalem representing heaven at one end, and Jericho (because it's so low-lying and hot!) hell at the other. The man is travelling in the wrong direction, and is therefore attacked, robbed and left for dead. It is in this oppressed condition that the redeemer finds him, to bring him out of slavery to freedom (exodus), here signified by the inn (standing for the community of the Church which cares for the disciples of Jesus until He comes again).

Born in the wrong country

Canaan might have been the land of promise, but for four hundred years the chosen people, including their redeemer Moses, were born in Egypt. Heaven is our true home as God's children, yet all of us, including our redeemer Jesus Christ, were born in exile, far from home. Egypt symbolizes the world without God, and it is a very good symbol. It is a tiny strip of land in the north-east of Africa, divided naturally into two by the river Nile. It was forever in conflict between life and death, represented respectively by the Nile and the desert. What made Egypt fertile was the overflowing of the Nile, but, as we know from the story of Joseph in Genesis, this did not always happen: then the desert had the upper hand and famine ensued. Egypt worshipped her river as the source of her life. She created a great civilization and built great monuments, as if she was destined to make her mark on this world only. Thousands of years later these monuments are still the pride of the world. The Egyptians embalmed their dead, hoping to make them immortal – we can see them today along with their Book of the Dead. Egypt left a testimony to death after her: *sic transit gloria mundi*.

Canaan was not like this: no great monuments or civilization or wonderful achievements to show. It was a land where God's people would have to live in total dependence on Him for survival. It has always been, and still is, God's way, to bring His people to a place of total dependence on Him. It is only when we live in this total obedience to His will that the blessings flow (epitomized by the promise of 'milk and honey'). Yet this little 'nothing' land, this tiny region on the east side of the Mediterranean, gave us the life and light of the world in Christ – the one who conquered death and left us an empty tomb as His witness. And through her also a book has come down to us, the Book of Life, the scriptures.

Serving the wrong master

Exodus 1:8. 'Then a new king who knew nothing of Joseph came to power in Egypt.' At first sight it seems incredible that a Pharaoh would not have heard of Joseph or his good work for the country. But let us look into it. About 1550 BC the Egyptians expelled the Hykos dynasty from Egypt. That dynasty were of semitic origin and had dominated the country since about 1760 BC. They had arrived in Egypt in similar circumstances to Jacob's family, had risen to power and eventually ruled the land. It is understandable that a king of semitic origin would have been favourable to Joseph and his family; but, with a change of dynasty, Egyptian hatred turned on all semites, including those living in the Nile delta where Jacob's descendants were.

This new line of kings may have been of foreign origin also: it says in Isaiah (52:4), 'My people went down at the first into Egypt to sojourn there, and the Assyrian oppressed them for nothing' (RSV:CB). Seti I ruled from c.1309–1290 BC and the oppression began under him. It was continued by his successor Rameses II (1290–1224 BC), who was most likely the Pharaoh of the exodus. This nineteenth dynasty of Pharaohs was most uneasy at the presence of the twelve non-native tribes who were growing so fast. 'But the Israelites were fruitful and prolific. They became so numerous and strong that the land was filled with them' (Exodus 1:7f). They were seen as a threat, as possible allies of warlike invaders. This generated fear, and so the Israelites found their privileged status removed, then their rights, then even their freedom: finally they were pressed into slavery and hard labour.

King Rameses II had moved his residence to the Nile delta and there set up massive building programmes, using the Hebrew slaves as his cheap labour force. Exodus 1:11 says that 'in this way they built the store-cities of Pithom and Rameses for Pharaoh'. This was political expediency on Pharaoh's part and might well have succeeded in a world without God, but Pharaoh had not reckoned on the presence of the unseen God with His people, the Lord, the living God. Nor had he reckoned on the power of faith among the Hebrews. Without realizing it he had entered into a holy war with God, a war which would humble his pride, bring his country to the brink of ruin, and cost him the life of his firstborn son and heir.

It is dangerous to fight the living God. 'If this enterprise,' it is written in the Acts of the Apostles (5:39), 'this movement of theirs, is of human origin it will break up of its own accord; but if it does in fact come from God you will not only be unable to destroy them, but you might find yourselves fighting against God.' These wise words from Gamaliel to the Jewish Sanhedrin some fifteen hundred years later about the new people of God, the Christians, might have helped Pharaoh in a similar situation. But Pharaoh had no such advice and so found himself caught up in the greatest drama of the Old Testament – on the wrong side!

In the great historical and spiritual drama which was about to unfold, Pharaoh represents the great adversary of God's people, the devil. By reflecting on his behaviour towards the people we will learn what the scriptures are trying to say about the real enemy. The picture will become clearer as we go along, but here we see that he initially deprived God's people of their freedom – and this typifies the work of the devil, who seduced mankind into sin (Genesis 3) which is spiritual slavery, thus depriving us of our God-given freedom. All of us have been born into original sin and its consequences, and labour under the burden of our own, and other people's, sins, in a broken and bruised world. But into this situation came Jesus as deliverer and saviour, with His invitation to the slaves of sin: 'Come to me, all you who labour and are overburdened, and I will give you rest. Shoulder my yoke and learn from me, for I am gentle and humble in heart, and you will find rest for your souls. Yes, my yoke is easy and my burden light' (Matthew 11:28f). The language used here by St Matthew is the language of the exodus. Redemption involves a change of master or lord. Is it to be the cruel enemy or the kind saviour? The choice is ours.

Redemption not only involves a change of master, but also a change of kingdom. It involves changing from the kingdom of this world to the kingdom of our Lord and of His Christ. In Exodus this means exchanging Egypt for Canaan, not an easy transition as we shall see in all the struggles in the wilderness, and some do not make it at all. The Hebrews first – then all those who want to be saved after them – will have to learn to put their trust in God and allow Him to lead them out of darkness into His wonderful light. This liberation was first proclaimed by Moses, and later reached its glorious fulfilment in Christ.

God was about to reveal Himself to *all* Egypt, as the true master and sovereign Lord of history; He was about to demonstrate His power and protection over the people who chose Him as Lord, to show Himself almighty in the plagues. The people will be able to distinguish the two masters clearly and therefore be in a position to choose. God will not force Himself on anyone, whether Egyptian or Israelite, but *will* reveal Himself to all, for 'God wants all men to be saved and come to the knowledge of the truth'. Later on (Exodus 12:38) we will discover that others living in Egypt besides the Israelites chose, in the end, to follow the Lord and His servant Moses. God was heard.

The faith of the people of Israel
Exodus 1:15–20. It was under Seti I that the oppression began, so it was probably he who decided to take steps to counteract the population explosion among the Hebrews. He ordered the midwives to kill all boys at birth, while letting the girls live. His problem is summed up thus (Exodus 1:12f): 'But the more they were crushed, the more they increased and spread, and men came to dread the sons of Israel.' There are important principles here that have been illustrated all down the ages.

(i) There is the hatred of the 'world' for the people of God. By 'world' I do not mean this lovely planet that God has given us to live in. I am not denying the magnificent beauty of nature which manifests God's presence and glory to us – No! I mean life as lived by those who act as if God is not with us . . . and suffer the consequent misery and corruption that spoils God's world. Witness the persecutions against the Church in every generation.

(ii) Then the people of the world persecute the people of God. 'If they persecuted me, they will persecute you too' we find in John's gospel (15:20).

(iii) But this very persecution (in this instance, slavery) purifies the sons of God, strengthens their faith, and throws them back into total dependence on God – as is shown in Psalm 119:67, 'Before I was afflicted I went astray, but now I hold to your promise'. Suffering is one of God's most effective instruments, if we allow it to do its purifying work. It detaches us from the world, refines us 'like gold in the furnace' (Sirach 2:5). Later in their history, when they reflect on their experiences in Egypt, they will call it 'the furnace of Egypt' (Deuteronomy 4:20).

(iv) Suffering makes them a strong people, almost invincible. We say that the blood of the martyrs is the seed of the Church – so, not only does suffering not destroy the people of God, it actually improves them! Dare I say it? It is good for them! Here in Exodus we see that this hardy race of slaves are not only not being crushed, they are increasing and multiplying and filling the land, so that Pharaoh felt that the only solution was to exterminate them. Tyrants throughout history, even to our own day, have felt the same. This plan of his to kill off the race that was to bring forth the Messiah is one of Satan's oldest ploys. It began in Genesis (3:15): 'I will put enmity between you and the woman, between your offspring and hers; He will strike your head, while you strike at his heel.'

The eternal enmity between Satan and his representatives (here Pharaoh) and the woman (the nation of Israel) and her offspring (the Messiah) is foretold here at the dawn of history. The ultimate victory for the Messiah is clearly stated, namely that He will crush the head of the serpent. The scriptures provide us with several examples of the enemy striking at the nation of Israel to kill it off, to prevent the saviour being born. Here Pharaoh decided on a massacre of male infants. Why did he not kill off the adults as well? Well, one very good reason was that it was time for Moses, the redeemer of the exodus, to be born! Secondly the adults were, for the time being, his cheap labour force.

You will find the same pattern in St Matthew. In chapter 2 (vv. 16–19) King Herod, another representative of the enemy, decides on exactly the same procedure, the massacre of the baby boys at Bethlehem; only this time it is much more serious as it is an attempt to kill off the Messiah Himself. In neither case did the enemy succeed, because he was up against the faith of a fervent few who were totally committed to the Lord and who would do His will at any price, even their own deaths. It is amongst these that we must count the Hebrew midwives, as women who feared God. They knew the living God and reverenced Him, and would not break His law (which was written only on their hearts at this stage). They risked civil disobedience in order to be faithful to God. Like the rest of us, they had to choose between the tangible and the invisible God. Pharaoh's soldiers, prisons and the possibility of torture would have swayed lesser souls – but not Shiprah and Puah, whose names mean 'beauty' and 'splendour', two lovely jewels for God. It seems that the might of Pharaoh could not hold out against them, and God gave them wisdom to answer the king (Exodus 1:15–21). The power of heroic faith is so great that it commands respect even in one's enemy: so we find that the women were not punished. Indeed God rewarded them for their obedience to Him by blessing them with families of their own. It is interesting that their reward from God was in this life, real and tangible.

Open conflict

The brave action of the Hebrew midwives forced Pharaoh to come out into the open. He turned to all his own subjects, who were obviously not Israelites, and ordered them to throw the Hebrew boys into the Nile. It was now no longer a struggle between Pharaoh and the Hebrews, but between Pharaoh with all his people, and God with all His people. This was holy war. The battle lines were drawn up, and God would intervene to initiate the exodus of His people from slavery to freedom.

2. The Cry of the Poor

By the time we move into chapter two of Exodus the
Israelites are the poor of the land, with no human rights,
and treated most harshly by their oppressors. It was then
that they turned to the God of their ancestors, and
discovered in their own experience that He was still with
them, and was willing to listen to them, and respond to
them. Unknown to them (as yet), God had called this
people to bear witness before the world to the unseen but
ever-present Living God. It was their task, under His
guidance, to reveal Him to the world; and their knowledge
of Him was not to be theoretical but experiential. Their
great boast before the world was that God was with them.

God-with-us

From the beginning God had told their ancestors 'I will be
with you'. The whole story of Abraham was that of a man
who walked with God. God was with him as his guide
(Genesis 12:1–2), as his protection (15:1), as the God of
promise and covenant (chapter 17), as the God who reveals
Himself to men (chapter 18). This revelation continued for
Isaac (26:24) and Jacob. God revealed Himself to Jacob
(28:10–22) in the same way. They were to go forward into
the unknown future with the security of God's promise 'I
am with you' (28:15). He, too, experienced God's guiding
hand in his everyday life (31:3), and God's personal
revelation of Himself to him (35:1–15) and the assurance
of His protective presence, when he feared to go down into
Egypt (46:2–5).

Now the people as a whole were to discover God-with-us

when they turned to Him in their troubles. Later, they sang in the Psalms:

The face of the Lord frowns on evil men,
to wipe their memory from the earth;
the eyes of the Lord are turned towards the virtuous,
his ears to their cry.

They cry for help and the Lord hears
and rescues them from all their troubles;
The Lord is near to the broken-hearted,
He helps those whose spirit is crushed.

(Psalm 34:16–18)

High over all nations, the Lord!
His glory transcends the heavens!
Who is like the Lord our God?
enthroned so high, He needs to stoop
to see the sky and earth!

He raises the poor from the dust;
He lifts the needy from the dunghill
to give them a place with princes,
with the princes of his people.

(Psalm 113:4–8)

It is their testimony, sung in psalm and told in the narrative that makes up the Old Testament scriptures, that forms their declaration to the world of who God is, for them as well as for anyone else who cares to go seeking after the Lord, the Living God.

This theme of God-with-us does not stop with the exodus. It goes right through the history of this people, on into the New Testament era, and on down to our own day and our own experience of the Lord. His revelation to Moses at the Burning Bush will be dealt with separately but it did not end with Moses. Joshua, who took over the leadership of this people after Moses, discovered that God continued with *him*: 'As long as you live, no one shall be able to stand in your way: I will be with you as I was with

Moses: I will not leave you or desert you' (Joshua 1:5,9). It went on with the Judges also (Judges 6:16; 11:29; 13:25), and the Kings and Prophets (cf. Jeremiah 1:8, Isaiah 6:1–10), all those who had special responsibility over God's people.

But God was with *this nation* also in a special way, and this is what distinguished her from *all* other nations, and made her very special, and a witness for God among the nations of the earth. 'If you are not going with us yourself, do not make us leave this place. By what means can it be known that I, I and my people, have won your favour, if not by your going with us? By this we shall be marked out, I and my people, from all the peoples on the face of the earth' (Exodus 33:15–16). God's special presence with His people was their mark of election – their claim to be 'Sons of God'. They knew that when God was with them no enemy could withstand them (Joshua 2:24) but if God was *not* with them – if He withdrew His presence because of their disobedience – then they could, and would, be conquered by their enemies (Joshua 12). The whole Book of Jeremiah testifies to this (cf. 6:19–21, Lamentations 1:14). The greatest punishment for them would be for God to remove His presence from them (cf. Psalm 51:11, Lamentations 5:21–22, Jeremiah 44: 20–23).

The Tabernacle in the Wilderness was to become the first 'home' for God on earth, where His Presence would be manifested in the Cloud.

Then God's home moved to Shiloh and finally to Jerusalem, the City of God. God's glory descended on the Temple after its consecration by Solomon (1 Kings 8:10–13); and Jerusalem became 'the Holy City', a symbol of Heaven – the place where God lives and reigns.

The future Messiah was to be called 'Immanuel' – God-with-us (Isaiah 7:14), and the New Testament era begins with God revealing Himself to Zechariah and Mary, and with God's assurance through the angel: 'I am with you' (Luke 1:29). Jesus is described in the gospels as a man who walked with God – the one on whom the Holy Spirit dwells

(John 1:33). He showed Himself to *be* God, revealing Himself fully to us in love, mercy and compassion, and He sent His disciples out on their mission to all the world with the same assurance that the Lord gave the Israelites of old: 'Know that I am with you always; yes, to the end of time' (Matthew 28:20; cf. Mark 16:20). The Christians now become the new people of God and carry the special presence of Jesus with them in the Eucharist and in the Word and in the Mystical Body. The Christian missionaries were to experience too that 'if God is for us, who can be against us?' (Romans 8:31).

This great 'I am' would eventually receive a response of adoration, praise, worship and service not only from the Jewish nation but from *all* nations!

But back in Exodus we just have an afflicted people, at the very dawn of their history, crying out to the Lord in their pain. They had no idea what God's plans were for them in the future, but they would discover Him step by painful step.

> The sons of Israel, groaning in their slavery,
> cried out for help and from the depths of their
> slavery their cry came up to God.
> God heard their groaning and he called to
> mind his covenant with Abraham, Isaac and Jacob.
> (Exodus 2:23–24)

The Hebrew slaves had many lessons to learn before they could enter into a new relationship with God. One of the first of these lessons was the difference between 'groaning' and 'crying out to God' in prayer, and this lesson has to be re-learned in every life, and by every group of people who wish to enter into deep relationship with God. To groan and complain is easy. Self-pity comes naturally to us, yet it does not motivate us to change the circumstances that we complain about. But to cry out to God for help in genuine prayer means that you are willing to co-operate with whatever changes are necessary to solve the problem.

Prayer that demands a magical response from God, or a 'quick and easy' solution, does not indicate the openness God needs in any situation to work out His own designs. To kill off the Pharaoh might seem to be the easy solution (2:23), but the Israelites found to their cost that his successor (Ramesis II) was just as bad. No. The true answer to prayer was to let God intervene in His own way, to bring His own solution, which would be a permanent one for all concerned, and would enable Israel to become all that God called her to be. In our own lives we find it just as difficult as the Hebrews to let God have His way with us, and work out His own designs with us and through us, so that the ambition He has for us (like a good Father) can be fully realized in us. We will learn much from the pain and struggles of this people that will enlighten our own.

One of the reasons why we resist God's answer to our troubles is because He apparently takes so long to provide those answers. During all the groaning and crying out of the years of slavery, Moses, the redeemer, had to be born, to grow up, to be educated and prepared for His mission. In all the time this took it must have seemed to the poor slaves that their prayers were not being heard in the heavens! But God did hear (2:24). To the modern mind this delay is intolerable. The 'instant' generation finds it very difficult to grasp. We expect God to respond with a quick and painless solution, like many of our modern remedies. But the Sovereign Lord of the Universe behaves very differently, and one of our most difficult tasks is just to learn 'His ways'. When we look back at the solution He gave to Israel in Egypt we see the wisdom and the wonder of it, but I doubt whether many of the poor slaves saw either – as we shall see later! Many of them had to live and die without seeing the results of their prayers. They, like us, were called to believe without seeing, and to trust in the goodness of God towards all His creatures.

3. God's Answer

A deliverer is born

Exodus 2:1 introduces us to a family from the tribe of Levi, whom God had chosen to give His answer to the prayer of His people. The parents were Amran and Jochabed (6:20) and they had three children, Miriam, Aaron and Moses; all of them were to be used by God to lead the new nation of Israel. Moses was called to become the deliverer, leader and lawgiver; Aaron was to become the first High Priest; Miriam was to help in saving Moses' life as a child and to become a co-leader with her brothers later, as well as becoming a prophetess (cf. Exodus 15:20f; Numbers 12:1–15).

They were obviously a family of great faith, who put their trust in God to deal with all the ordinary, everyday events of their lives. They not only asked God to intervene but *allowed* Him to do so in order to help them. This is the important difference between them and all the other Hebrew families. The principle is exactly the same for us. Many people claim to believe in and trust God, but do not allow Him to come close to them and intervene in their everyday affairs. They seem to be afraid to let God come near. There is a gap between what they believe and what they do.

This is what makes saints: they allow God to come close and reveal Himself in the minutiae of everyday life. Therefore they have the strength and the grace to deal with life where others fail.

The edict of Pharaoh was still in operation when Moses was born (1:22); according to this Moses was to be thrown into the river Nile. The family hid the child as long as possible (2:3) (Hebrews 11:23), but when they could no longer do so, they made him a papyrus basket, coating it with bitumen and pitch to keep the water out. They placed their beloved child in this basket and put him carefully among the reeds at the water's edge, so that the basket would not float away. Miriam, his sister, was left hiding nearby, keeping watch (vv. 2–4) to see what would happen to him.

This touching story tells us both about obedience to authority – Pharaoh – and about trust in the Lord, the unseen but ever-present God who does not want His children massacred in this or any other way.

Moses' mother put her child in the place of death in obedience to her ruler, but she trusted the Lord to intervene on her behalf and save the baby, which only God could do.

This incident was the key for the rest of the people that trust in God was the only way out for them too in their national crisis.

Pharaoh's daughter went down to bathe in the river that day with her attendants. She noticed the basket and sent her maid to fetch it. When she opened it she found the child crying, and had compassion on him even though she knew he was one of the Hebrew children. Then Miriam came out of her hiding place and offered to get a nurse to look after the child. When the princess agreed, Miriam brought back her own mother, who was paid by the princess to take care of the child until he was weaned (vv. 5–9). This ingenious solution which God gave to Jochabed should encourage all of us to let God *be* God, the Almighty One, for us in our personal and national affairs (cf. Romans 8:28f).

God's action in the rescue of Moses from the water – which was so simple! – is an eloquent comment on the folly of human wisdom (cf. Job 5:13). Pharaoh sought to destroy the Hebrew people from the face of the earth, but due to God's wisdom and action on behalf of Moses and his mother, Pharaoh had to feed, clothe, house and educate the very man who would set the Israelites free and cause his own downfall! (cf. 1 Corinthians 1:19, 3:18).

So far Pharaoh has been outwitted by brave and independent women, namely the midwives, Jochabed and Miriam – and now by his own daughter! This was already a poor record for a man whose pride was to reduce Egypt to ruin in the plagues.

Moses was back home with his family now, for three to four years, being cared for by his parents; in those days the weaning process took a long time. It was certainly long enough in God's design for this child to imbibe the lively faith of his family, and learn his identity as an Israelite. That Moses was afterwards to display such unshakable faith and trust in God shows that this experience of home must have been vital for him.

As a young boy then, maybe four or five years old, Moses was taken by his parents to Pharaoh's palace where he was treated as a son (2:10). It was Pharaoh's daughter who named him Moses, because she said, 'I drew him out of the water' – which is the meaning of the name (cf. Hebrews 11:24; Acts 7:21). Moses joined the other royal children in the palace school and was taught 'all the wisdom of the Egyptians and became a man with power both in speech and in actions' (Acts 7:22).

There is a strange yet wonderful thing here; we see in the case of Moses, and later of Daniel and other servants of God, that the safest place in time of trouble is in the lions' den, when God has shut the lions' mouths! (cf Daniel 6:17–26). There was such danger for the Hebrews in Egypt at this time that the only safe place for Moses to grow up was in Pharaoh's palace where no one would suspect him. Here Moses learned all that he needed to know when he returned many years later as God's envoy.

We have no information about the youth of Moses, but the letter to the Hebrews tells us that he did not lose his faith or his sense of identity with his own people, so it must have been instilled into him deeply as a small child (Hebrews 11:24). As an adult he rejected his royal identity in order to show solidarity with his own people

It was by faith that, when he grew to manhood, Moses refused to be known as the son of Pharaoh's daughter and chose to be ill-treated in company with God's people rather than to enjoy for a time the pleasures of sin. He considered that the insults offered to the Anointed. [i.e. the people of God] were something more precious than all the treasures of Egypt, because he had his eyes fixed on the reward . . . he held to his purpose like a man who could see the Invisible.

(Hebrews 11:24–27)

This decision was to cost Moses a great deal because his adoption by Pharaoh's daughter would have made him a legal son and heir to the royal family. But apart from the loss of the wealth, honour and glory of a prince, it was also a very dangerous decision as it constituted a threat to Pharaoh from within his own household.

Moses' sin and flight (Exodus 2:11–15)
Once the decision was made to identify with his own people, Moses set out to try to help them. He felt somehow that God would deliver them through him. 'He thought his brothers realized that through him God would liberate them, but they did not' (Acts 7:25). How he came to this decision we do not know. Maybe he thought that his position of influence as a prince would help them or he could put his education and wealth at their disposal. It seems from the text that he thought he could save them himself, in his own strength – in the 'flesh'. But he was about to learn that 'the flesh avails us nothing' (John 6:63). It was not as a prince or a man of importance that God would use Moses to save his people, but only when Moses had emptied himself of all worldliness and had become a true man of God, and a 'nothing' in his own eyes (v. 14).

The turning point in Moses' life – as in ours so often – was his greatest sin. In attempting to save one of the

Hebrew slaves Moses killed an Egyptian and hid his body in the sand (2:11–12). The following day he attempted to bring peace between two Hebrew slaves, but they would not accept his intervention after his violent action the day before (v. 13–14). So Moses discovered, to his cost, that his fanaticism had turned the Hebrews away from Him, and made him a fugitive from Egyptian justice. He was now a murderer on the run! This action of his made Pharaoh realize that Moses was an Israelite too, and he expelled him from court. So in one swift act of passion Moses lost all his privileges, status and rights. Pharaoh wanted to kill him, so Moses fled to the land of Midian (v. 15) (Numbers 22:4). The land of Midian lies south of Edom and to the east of the Gulf of Aqaba, so Moses went as far away as he could from Egypt. To reach this place he would have to cross the Sinai peninsula – alone. Moses was to spend many years in the desert of Midian where he learned God's way of action, which is very different to man's (cf. Zechariah 4:6b). He was to become well acquainted with the Sinai peninsula, which was useful later, as he was destined to lead the nation of Israel through the desert for forty years.

The desert a home

The scriptures illustrate for us time after time that God never abandons the sinner. God's love continues 'to seek out and save that which was lost'. We see this care for Adam and Eve after their sin, for Jacob (Genesis 3:28–30) and here for Moses. Jesus spoke about it in the parable of the prodigal son (Luke 15). Moses found himself a fugitive in the desert, but God used this fugitive's generosity and innate sense of justice to give him a home and security during his long desert experience. In an incident by a well, even though Moses was a stranger and a foreigner, he defended some shepherd girls who were the daughters of the local pagan priest and watered their sheep for them. This won him acceptance in the home of Reuel the priest (who is also called Jethro in 3:1, 4:18 and 18:1). Reuel means 'friend of God' and Jethro means 'abundance'. And so Moses, the Egyptian prince, became a shepherd in the desert. He had now become like his father Abraham – a wandering nomad – and his identification with his own people was complete.

This desert experience was to be vital in the preparation of this man for his great mission, but first of all he was comforted by the love of Zipporah, who was given to him in marriage, and, like Joseph before him, he brought forth two sons in exile. He also resembled Jacob who lived many years in exile tending his uncle Laban's flocks (cf. Genesis 29).

The school of the desert

We do not know how long Moses lived as a nomadic shepherd in the desert, but we are given to believe that it was a considerable length of time. He had long years to reflect and pray, and this changed him radically. Silence and stillness of the heart are great teachers if we only would listen to them: 'Be still and know that I am God' (Psalm 46:10). Far away from the din and turbulence of the great cities, the tinsel of material things loses its glamour; the world of people and affairs is viewed in a different light. The heart is not swollen with pride or ambition where it breathes the pure air of God's loving presence. More and more clearly as time passes the 'still small voice' (1 Kings 19:13) of the Lord is heard in a heart where the emotions have found their true balance and one responds gently to the invitation 'Come to Me . . . I will give you rest' (Matthew 11:28f). Neither the dress, status nor glory of an Egyptian prince means anything to a heart purified of ambition. The loss of wealth means nothing to a heart filled with heavenly treasure – the treasure that moth and thief cannot destroy.

The lessons Moses learned 'on the far side of the wilderness' (3:1) were some of the greatest in his life. He was radically changed; he became a man of prayer which was essential to his mission as a leader. To be God's representative to the chosen people Moses needed to be able to remain in God's presence for long periods, imbibing His love and learning His ways so that he could teach the people God's will.

Called by God (Exodus 3:1–6)

By the time God called Moses many years later this shepherd had become a nobody, a 'nothing' in the eyes of the world – long since forgotten by Egypt, except by his own family. God seemed to be in no hurry; He spent long years in the training of His envoy (cf. Psalm 90:4). But he was now purified 'a vessel fit for his master's use' (2 Timothy 2:21), and God's call came at a time and in a way that was very unexpected.

One day Moses noticed a bush burning, but this is not an unusual sight in the desert. In the great heat the poor shrubs can dry up like sticks and spontaneously ignite. No! What attracted his attention was the fact that the bush was burning, but was not being consumed! He was observing a scientific miracle. It was the fact that the bush survived the fire that drew Moses closer (v.2). God had caught his attention! It was then that a greater miracle manifested itself. God was in the heart of the fire! (cf. Deuteronomy 33:16), and He called to Moses from within the fire (v.4), but when Moses came closer in answer to the call, he was told to remove his sandals as a sign of reverence before the All-Holy God.

Then following a tradition He Himself had begun with the Patriarchs, God revealed Himself to Moses: 'I am the God of your father,' He said, 'the God of Abraham, Isaac and Jacob' (v.6). Suddenly Moses realized that he was face to face with the Lord, the unseen but ever-present, ever-living God, and he covered his face in fear.

The burning bush

What was it that Moses saw and experienced? God came

to him in the shape of a flame of fire, just as He did for the early Church on Pentecost Day (Acts 2). This miracle has great significance in understanding redemption. God gave Moses a visible sign to help his understanding, because he would have to face a people who could neither read or write, and God wanted to impress lessons upon their hearts that they would never forget.

There are two elements to deal with, namely the call of the Prophet and the message of Redemption.

The call of the Prophet
God called Moses in the midst of his everyday activities while he was tending his sheep. He came suddenly and unexpectedly, calling Moses by his name, thus claiming personal knowledge of him and lordship over him: 'I have called you by your name, you are mine' (Isaiah 43:1). God then revealed Himself to Moses and appointed this poor shepherd to be priest, prophet and king (i.e. law-giver and ruler) over Israel. Moses realized that he had been chosen for a great destiny and that his life must radically change. He also realized that God expected an immediate answer of surrender to His will, but Moses was not ready for that!

Moses knew that he was dealing with the God of the Covenant (2:24), a God who is always faithful to His side of the Covenant regardless of the unworthiness of His people. But God wanted an envoy to work through. When God made His Covenant with Abraham, Isaac and Jacob it was not because of any good he saw in them. No! It was His own sovereign goodness and mercy that made Him do it. So it is here with Moses. When God decided to deliver Israel and form another Covenant with Moses it was not due to any goodness in the Hebrew slaves, but because of His own mercy. The same principle holds true for the new Covenant which Jesus made with His Father on our behalf (cf. Titus 3:5).

The pattern that we see here in the call of Moses is

41

similar to that of other servants of God in scripture. For example, little Samuel was called suddenly in the night while he was still a child, and was commissioned for his future work (1 Samuel 3:1–21). Isaiah, Jeremiah and other prophets were called in this way also (cf. Isaiah 6:1–8; Jeremiah 1:4–10). The Apostles, too, heard the challenge of Jesus to 'come follow me' in the midst of their everyday activities, and Paul encountered Jesus as a heavenly light on the Damascus road (Mark 1:16–20; Acts 9:1–19).

It is in our normal everyday activities that we meet God. He is the God of the 'ordinary'. If we do not allow Him to meet us and help us here I do not know whether we will ever meet Him in any real sense. Any people who have ever allowed Him to 'come into' their lives have found themselves gradually transformed and their lives directed heavenwards (cf. Revelation 3:20). It is our ordinary activities, touched by God, that make the difference for those of us who try to live a spiritual life amidst the simple events that make up our general lives. The glory of God's presence is manifested to us, and through us to others, when we allow Him to catch our attention, and break in upon our lives. Then we, too, find ourselves in conversation with the God who calls us to become His true servants and to co-operate with Him in the redemption of suffering mankind.

The measure of redemption

It seems that God showed Himself to Moses in a burning thorn bush. The thorns would be a reminder, therefore, of the curse of sin (Genesis 3:18) which would demand the judgement of God. This is shown by the fire. The whole symbol would represent first the condition of sinful man before the All-Holy God before redemption, where his sinful condition demands judgement from God.

But how is it that this poor thorn bush survived the fire? It is because a second level of meaning is signified. The burning thorn bush foreshadows the saving work of Christ on Calvary. In his incarnation He became for us 'a root in arid ground' (Isaiah 53:2) (i.e. the thorn bush), but the fullness of the Godhead was in Him (Colossians 2:9) (i.e. God revealed in the thorn bush), Hence He was able to take upon Himself the fire of God's judgement for sin, and survive it (Luke 22:37). Therefore the burning bush represents the triumph of the Resurrection after Jesus went through death and hell to save us. On the cross Jesus wore the thorn bush – as a crown upon His head! (cf. Galatians 3:14). Jesus *is* the living Burning Bush, on fire with love and zeal for His Father's glory and for the redemption of mankind (cf. John 1:17). This burning love was the motive for His embracing the cross.

The living burning bush can also represent the nation of Israel before redemption. She was reduced to slavery, suffering 'in the furnace of Egypt' (Deuteronomy 4:20). This is the thorn bush on fire. But Israel was not destroyed by her experience because God was with her – God was in the heart of the fire.

The Lord *was* with His people – though unseen – and He was about to save them through Moses, the deliverer. A similar teaching is given in the Book of Daniel chapter 3, where three young men find themselves, because of their loyalty to the Lord, thrown into a fiery furnace. But God came to their rescue *in the fire* (vv. 49–50), and saved them from the heat of the fire so that they were untouched by it.

When things go wrong in our own lives we seem to demand that God either *remove* the circumstances or the people from us, or remove *us*! But that is not the way out (exodus!). He comes to us *in* our trouble, in the fire, and brings us salvation and help through the very circumstances that we thought should be removed. The God of the exodus goes on working in all our lives if only we will allow Him (cf. Isaiah 63:8–9).

There is yet another message in the burning bush! The thorn bush was nothing in itself. It was a useless thing, but God 'chooses the weak things of the world to confound the strong' (1 Corinthians 1:27). This useless bush represents the children of God throughout history – and ourselves too. We are not important of ourselves (cf. John 15:4–5). What makes us special is that the Lord, the living God, dwells with us! For us Christians this symbol is very precious because we have been made temples of the Living God (John 14:17; 1 Corinthians 3:16–17). God is with His Church as a whole, and with each member of it. So we see that God still manifests His glory to the unbelieving eyes of the world through that simple thorn bush, but now it is *us*, on fire with love and zeal for God and His people. The exodus has come full circle!

God's concern for His people

At this juncture God spoke to Moses of the very personal concern He had for His people in Egypt: He said that He had *seen* the miserable state of His people; that He had *heard* their prayer for deliverance; He was well aware of their sufferings and He was determined to save them. This means that the Lord was very much present during the long years of slavery and He felt compassion on their sufferings. God is the one, both in the Old and the New Testaments, who shows compassion for the suffering poor. To Him they are like sheep without a shepherd, and so he sets a shepherd over them: Moses first and then Jesus (cf. Jeremiah 50:6; Psalm 119:176; Matthew 9:36; Exodus 34:29).

In the Old Testament we see that the Father showed the same loving compassion to the people as Jesus, His incarnate Son, was to show His redemptive mission (cf. Hebrews 1:3). God is the same then and now, and He is anxious to save whenever the people are ready to let Him act on their behalf. But those who are held captive in the slavery of sin can be very unwilling to let God set them free. They love their sin even though it holds them bound, and that is why suffering may be necessary to disenchant them first – as we see happening among the slaves in Egypt – so that they will be willing to listen to God's Word and to allow the Redeemer to save them by His grace. It is often only when they are reduced to a state of real misery that they turn to God, as the whole history of Israel so eloquently points out (cf. Hosea 5:15; Amos 4:4–12). Jesus illustrated this clearly in the parable of the Prodigal Son, who only 'came to his senses' when he was reduced to real misery; only then did he begin the journey back to his father's house (Luke 15:14–17). The exodus for the individual and for the nation begins at this point.

This whole passage also points clearly to the incarnation of the Son of God. God saw the misery of the whole human race since the fall of Adam. He heard the cries of the saints, the prophets and the poor – the *anawim* – that came to Him all down the centuries, begging for deliverance and for a saviour. In the meantime the people laboured under the slavery to sin, with all its consequent misery. Finally Jesus came down from heaven personally to save us and to head the New Israel (the Church) as she set out on her pilgrim journey through history – her exodus – until she would reach the true promised land in Heaven.

The mission of Moses (3:7–20)
In response to the cry of the people God called Moses to be their redeemer. Moses was to go to Pharaoh and demand the release of all his cheap labour force! In human terms the plan sounded crazy, certainly unworkable, and Moses was not at all impressed: 'Who am I to go to Pharaoh?' (v. 11). A shepherd from the desert would not even get as far as the presence of this great king! God's response to Moses was, 'I shall be with you'. Moses was to content himself that he would not be alone, that the unseen God would be at his side. To a person of little faith this would be cold comfort, but to a man matured by long years of silence and prayer this promise is very real.

It is thus that God comforted his servants all down through the generations. The comment of scripture on its holy men is that 'they walked with God' (cf. Enoch in

Genesis 5:22–24; Noah in Genesis 6:9; the people in Malachi 2:6; the Christians in Revelation 3:4).

So Moses found himself in that royal line of servants of God who knew the intimate presence of God throughout their lives. It is not to be wondered at, therefore, that God accomplished great things in them and through them for His people.

Who are you, Lord? (3:13–15)

Moses must be sure of the Person who is communicating with him, so he asked God to identify Himself clearly. In the Old Testament 'the name' represents the whole person, and there was a strong belief that having possession of the name of a god gave you some power over him. You see this in the exorcisms carried out by Jesus in His ministry. He got possession of the name of the spirit before casting him (them) out (cf. Mark 5:9–10; Acts 9:5). God responded by saying, 'I am who I am' (*ego eimi*), 'tell them "I am" sent you' (v.14). God was here speaking to Moses about His unseen presence with His people – that He is 'God-with-us' whom they already knew. He would show them step by step in their troubled history what a wonderful gift it was to have God so near: 'What great nation is there that has its gods *so near* as the Lord our God is to us whenever we call him?' (Deuteronomy 4:7, 12:5).

'My people will therefore know my name; that day they will understand that it is I who say, "I am here"' (Isaiah 52:6). It was to take them thousands of years to know the full implications of *ego eimi*. In fact it was not until Jesus came that *ego eimi* was spelled out for us, before our wondering eyes, in St John's gospel. Here we see Jesus reveal Himself as the Person who spoke to Moses – but now incarnate, now come Himself to save us! 'I am (*ego eimi*) the bread of life . . . I am the Light of the World . . . I am the *Good* Shepherd . . . I am the true vine . . . I am *He* . . . I am the Resurrection and the Life . . . I am the gate . . . Yes, I am a King . . . I am the Way, the Truth and the Life.'

This Living God was offering Himself as the guide and teacher of His people, as their food (manna) and life (water from the rock). He wanted to be their provider and their Father, their healer (in the bronze serpent) and their constant companion, and so it is still with us. The great 'I am' is still 'I am' for us today, and wants to be with us and work with us and through us by the operation of His Holy Spirit indwelling us. Our privilege is, in fact, much greater than theirs for He lives *within* us.

The revelation of the great 'I am' was a wonderful beginning to a marvellous pilgrimage of God's people throughout history, and this God was also the God of Abraham, Isaac and Jacob (3:15).

A hesitant hero

It was now God's time for action, 'now is the hour of salvation . . .' (Isaiah 49:8; 2 Corinthians 6:2). The long years of preparation for Moses were over, and the reign of God was to begin. But Moses had lost all interest in Egypt, and also, apparently, in saving the Israelites, and God had to motivate him strongly to go. Being uprooted from his desert life did not appeal to him, for he resisted change and insecurity, as all of us do.

He saw difficulties everywhere: (a) in the Hebrews, (b) in himself, and (c) in the mission. 'What if they will not believe me, or listen to my words [as happened before!] and say to me "The Lord has not appeared to you"!' This is a very real problem, and it shows Moses as a man in contact with reality. He could not imagine the people accepting this visionary nomad arriving in from the wilderness with some crazy notion about deliverance, when he has no authority or power or influence in the political or financial world (gone was the hastiness of youth). The solitude of the desert had sobered him indeed!

God's answer to Moses' objection was 'I will be with you', and in case this was not enough He assured him of the success of his mission (Isaiah 46:10). 'After you have led the people out of Egypt, you are to offer worship to God on this mountain.' God told him they would meet again together on Mt Sinai (or Horeb) – afterwards called 'the mountain of God' (3:1).

The Christian missionaries, challenged by Jesus a thousand years later to 'go into the whole world and preach the Gospel to every living creature', also needed to hear the comforting assurance of Jesus 'and behold I will be with you in all the days that are coming . . .' He also assured them of the success of their task: 'the gates of Hell will not prevail . . .' (Matthew 16:18).

The mission (3:16–20)
Moses was to gather the elders of the Israelites and tell them all that had happened, that their prayer for help had been heard, and that God had visited His people through Moses. They were to go to Pharaoh as a body of men representing their people and request leave to go on a three-day journey into the wilderness to offer sacrifice to God. Pharaoh would refuse, and then the whole drama of the exodus would begin.

One would not need a great deal of insight to know why Pharaoh would refuse to allow his entire slave labour force to go away for three days. For one thing it would bring his building plans to a complete halt, and he also knew that a three-day journey for these resident aliens would put them entirely outside his territory; he would no longer have jurisdiction over them. It would be a mass exodus from his country, and right now they were valuable to him.

The miraculous signs
Moses felt that he could not face the journey back to Egypt armed only with visions and words. He needed something to convince the people, and Pharaoh, that he was a sober man with a real mission. God, in His mercy, condescended

to give him three signs, and each sign carried vital information for this mission. The 'signs' here, as later in John's gospel, are miracles which testify to who the saviour is and the nature of his work. They carry a deep revelation hidden in the sign itself. They would be his credentials before Israel just as the miracle ministry of Jesus was to be later in their history. In both cases the prophet had to *prove* that he came from God (cf. John 6:30–31).

The first sign – the rod (4:3–5)
God told Moses to throw his staff on the ground; when he did it turned into a snake. God commanded Moses to catch it by the tail, and *in Moses' hand* it turned back into a staff, a rod. Either this is a useless trick that God gave to Moses, or it is a meaningful sign. If it is a trick then we are looking at our glorious God in the role of a magician! If it is a sign, then it befits the Lord to reveal Himself this way.

The serpent is a symbol of the enemy – the devil (cf. Genesis 3). The rod or staff was a shepherd's support in his long daily treks through the desert. Psalm 23 speaks of the shepherd – as God – protecting us with his rod and staff. So the staff is a symbol of God's grace. The lesson here, firstly, is that if Moses leans on God's grace (staff in hand) he can go forward successfully on his perilous mission, but if he goes in his own strength (as he did before, when he killed the Egyptian) he will be helpless before the enemy (the rod turned serpent). This lesson was taught by Jesus later in John 15:5 'without me you can do nothing'. Moses, and all the servants of God who followed him in history, had to learn this simple lesson – lean on God for your support and help; keep your eyes on the Lord! Peter learned it the hard way one stormy night on the Sea of Galilee (cf. Matthew 14:22–23). From now on this staff of Moses' was called 'the staff of God' (4:20). It will be important in the plagues and all the significant actions of Moses – a sign that Moses' power to work miracles came from God, and that the glory would be given to the right

Person (cf. Acts 3:12f). 'Staff-in-hand' will become the slogan for going forward under obedience to God.

The second half of the lesson shows us Moses reducing the serpent to a rod again. This signifies his role as God's chosen redeemer. He was to reduce the enemy to nothing under God's powerful action and guidance. It carried a great message for the Hebrews also and, indeed, for us. They were to see that their physical slavery symbolized a deeper, more terrible bondage – the slavery to sin (2 Timothy 2:26). This means that they were powerless before the might of the enemy, but God was coming to their help by sending them a redeemer through whom the enemy would be overcome and they would be set free. Jesus was the true saviour who would overcome the power of the devil on Calvary and so free the spiritual slaves who truly desired to be free of their chains (Luke 23:43). Like Moses, Jesus would not *force* us to follow Him into freedom and the Promised Land (cf. John 6:67).

The second sign – the leprous hand (4:6–7)

God told Moses to put his perfectly healthy hand into his bosom and when he drew it out it was leprous! And Moses now experienced not fear of the serpent as in the first sign – but fear of himself! God instructed him to put his hand back into his bosom and draw it out again – completely healed. Again, this is either magic or a sign.

Leprosy has always been seen by the Hebrews (Isaiah 1:4–6) as a sign or symbol of sin (cf. Leviticus 13, 14), and Moses was made to look at the leprosy of the human heart here – in other words, his eyes were opened to the need for redemption. He had to acknowledge the corruption that was within himself and his people, just as each one of us must do (cf. Mark 7). Jesus spoke eloquently of this during his ministry, when He accused the Pharisees of being full of 'every kind of corruption' in their hearts (Matthew 23:27). God knows that we must face our need for redemption before we will repent. Moses was being told that the real problem for the Israelites, and all others, lies in our own corrupt hearts and desires. This is a sober message, but necessary if we are to agree to co-operate with the process of salvation.

The Lord wanted to go to the root of the problem and save us, not just from outward slavery, but from inner bondage also. He would go to the very root of the problem, as Jesus demonstrated in the healing of the paralytic man in Mark. He freed the man from within first (Mark 2:6) and then from without (Mark 2:12). The inner freeing is the greater one, and the outer one merely points to it. Even so the freeing of Israel from Egypt points to the greater event that happened through Jesus our saviour in liberating all peoples from inner slavery – and from outward slavery if His royal law of love were lived out among us.

The healing of the leprous hand signifies the work of Jesus, our Redeemer, who is All-Holy in Himself (Hebrews 4:15; 1 Peter 2:22) yet took our sins upon Himself (2 Corinthians 5:21; 1 Peter 2:24) – thus becoming for a time 'the leper or leprous hand' for us. He paid the full penalty for sin on the cross – took our sins (leprosy) away from us, thus restoring us completely (the healed hand) (1 John 3:5). So the whole sign of the leprous hand shows us God's plan of redemption.

The third sign – The river of blood (4:8–9)
The first two signs should have been eloquent enough to show that Moses was God's special envoy, but just in case the signs were not accepted – and God shows here how well He knows us! – Moses was given a third. The third sign would amount to a declaration of war, and did, in fact, become the first plague.

Moses was instructed to take some water from the river and pour it on the ground, where it would turn into blood. This sign was to be given in Egypt, so the river in question is the Nile – which represents the life-blood of the nation. It was a warning of divine judgement if God was not listened to. Their life (Nile) would be turned into death (blood). It also contained a spiritual message, that the sinful worldly way they were living would end in real death – eternal death. As St Paul put it, 'the wages of sin is death' (Romans 6:23) – the fruit of a life of sin is death.

It is significant that this third sign was only to be given if the other two were refused. It was not God's way to threaten or terrify, but He would warn the people of the consequences of their actions if they did not listen to His merciful invitation to come to freedom in His great plan for them.

Moses was now armed with a great mission from God and with signs to prove that he really was His envoy, but it seems that the more he heard the less he wanted to go; he put up a huge resistance to God. The prospect of all that lay ahead for him made the quiet life of a shepherd very attractive indeed!

His first excuse was that he was not a good speaker. Like many a servant of God after him he felt inadequate for the task and used this as an excuse to resist grace, but behind his excuse we can see human pride that does not want to be made to look foolish. Most of us would stop short at being made 'fools for Christ's sake' (1 Corinthians 4:10). We want to look good and sound intelligent before the world, and this blocks the work of grace in us. St Paul learned a hard lesson on this in Athens when he, too, fell into the trap of using human rhetoric and philosophical reasoning in order to explain the mystery of Christ to the unbelievers (cf. Acts 17). He left Athens a humbled and chastened man, and spoke afterwards about his experience to the Corinthians (cf. 1 Corinthians 2:1–5).

The task before Moses now was that he should go before Pharaoh relying on God alone for his message, his power, his direction and his success, but this scared him, and he suggested that God choose someone else – *anyone* else! (4:13). To talk about relying on God is one thing, but actually to do it in practice is something human nature resists. We prefer to rely on ourselves, and on our own intelligence and powers. So God humbled Himself again to help His reluctant envoy and appointed Aaron, his older brother, to help him in his mission. It would enhance Moses' importance before Pharaoh and the people if he had a spokesman (cf. Acts 14:12), so we find that Aaron had already been called by God for his mission as spokesman now and as high priest later. In fact he had already left Egypt to go searching for Moses in the wilderness – even before Moses had finally agreed to God's plans! (4:14–17).

It is wonderful to see God at work in both men, preparing each one to meet the other, so that they can take on the leadership of Israel together. In just this way (Acts 9) Ananias and Saul receive visions at the same time which prepare them to meet each other, so that Saul (afterwards St Paul) could be received into the Church. In the case of Philip and the eunuch (Acts 8) and Cornelius and Peter (Acts 10) we again see the same principle at work.

There is a marked contrast between the resistance of Moses to God's plans for him and the wonderful obedience and surrender of Jesus, our true redeemer, to His Father. Quoting Psalm 40:6–8 the writer to the Hebrews tells us that Jesus' attitude on coming into the world was this:

> . . . . then I said just as I was commanded in
> the scroll of the book;
> God here I am! I am coming to obey your will
> (Hebrews 10:5–7)

The gospels give us an eloquent comment on His loving surrender to His Father throughout His life. His first recorded words were, 'Did you not realize that I must be about my Father's affairs?' (Luke 2:49). His final statement before His death was, 'It is finished' (John 19:30). In between these two extremes we have many statements made during His ministry to show the motive behind all His work: 'My aim is to do, not my own will, but the will of Him who sent me' (John 5:30). 'I always do what pleases Him' (John 8:30) (cf. also John 6:39f; 8:28, 38, 40, 55; 12:50).

The final statement of his commitment is this, '. . . the world must be brought to know that *I love the Father* and that I am doing exactly what the Father told me' (John 14:31).

Moses sets out for Egypt (4:18–31)

At long last Moses' resistance had been worn down. With the promise of help from Aaron he finally surrendered to God and made the necessary preparations. He took leave of his father-in-law Jethro and set out for Egypt with his wife and two sons. He ran into serious trouble immediately because his son was not circumcised. Until the new covenant was made in Sinai Moses was bound to the Abrahamic covenant which demanded the circumcision of all males (cf. Genesis 17:9–16). The Lord met him on the way and tried to kill him – which was a strange action if Moses was to act as His representative, but God is the God of Covenant, and always keeps the terms of Covenant; Moses could not represent Him before the people unless he formally entered into the Abrahamic Covenant, and the terms of the Covenant demanded that any uncircumcised male should be cut off from his people (Genesis 17:14). There is no record of Moses himself being circumcised, although it is difficult to see why his parents would neglect such an important act when they were so god-fearing.

'And the Lord let him live': once Moses obeyed the Covenant he could proceed with his journey. But he seems to have sent Zipporah and the two boys back home to Midian, as they disappear from the account at this point (4:26).

Soon afterwards Moses and Aaron met in the desert, a wonderful meeting after so many years apart. They shared God's plans with each other and together they returned to Egypt with the good news of redemption for the Hebrew slaves.

They gathered the elders of the people together in Goshen, and told them all that had occurred and what God planned to do for them. Moses performed miraculous signs for the people. They were convinced and accepted Moses and Aaron as the envoys of the Lord and rejoiced at this wonderful visitation of God to His people. Then, for the first time in this great saga, the people bent in reverent worship, awe and gratitude before God, their unseen friend and saviour and merciful Lord. God had told Moses the people would accept him – and they did! (cf. 3:18).

We see now, at this point, that during all the years while God prepared Moses for his mission, He was also preparing Israel for Moses. Now the moment was upon them. Moses was ready; Israel was ready to be saved and God's providential time had come.

II. The Time of Deliverance

4. Facing the Enemy

'My power is at best in weakness' (2 Corinthians 12:9). Jesus said this to St Paul in the midst of his mission, and it illustrates what we are about to witness in Moses' struggle with Pharaoh. We have already seen Moses' weakness; we are about to witness the wonders God worked through this poor instrument.

The first interview with Pharaoh

Moses and Aaron now faced their first appointment with Pharaoh, the powerful king of Egypt. They went before him and faithfully delivered God's message:

> This is what the Lord, the God of Israel, has said, 'Let my people go, so that they may keep a feast in the wilderness in honour of me' . . . Give us leave to make a three days' journey into the wilderness to offer sacrifice to the Lord our God, or he will come down on us with a plague or with the sword!
>
> (Exodus 5:1–60)

This was their first encounter with the enemy and it turned out – like all the subsequent ones – to be highly unpleasant. Pharaoh despised the Hebrews and was ill disposed towards their request.

The confrontation which was now beginning was to show

up the hearts of both opponents – uncovering, in the end, the humility and obedience of Moses before God, and the stubborn, rebellious, faithless heart of the king.

God always uses the ordinary events of our lives to show each of us what lies in our hearts (cf. Deuteronomy 8:2–6). If we are open to learn we will gain the valuable self-knowledge which is essential to personal growth. If we refuse to learn from the events of everyday life we become more and more hardened in our sinful attitudes and behaviour until our character has become fixed – incorrigible. We see this in Pharaoh, while at the same time Moses grows to spiritual maturity.

It was not unreasonable three thousand years ago to request time off work to worship one's God! Everyone worshipped some, if not many, gods. But Pharaoh was no fool. He saw at once that Moses and Aaron might, in fact, be planning a mass exodus from the country, and that he was in danger of losing his valuable slaves! This would bring all his great building projects to a standstill. So he gave a clear refusal to the request (5:2–3).

Firstborn among the nations

Moses' request reflected the call of Israel to become God's 'firstborn son' among the nations (4:22). She was the first nation to be asked to enter into a covenant relationship with God, and to be His instrument to set up the Kingdom of God on earth. She was to be the nation above all others who would worship the Lord, and Him alone (4:22f). She was called to come out from the world of unbelief – represented by Egypt – and become 'a consecrated nation, a people set apart (therefore holy) to sing the praises of God' (Deuteronomy 7:6). St Peter told the early Christians that this was their call, too, since the spiritual exodus of the People of God in the New Testament was based on the exodus of Israel from Egypt (cf. 1 Peter 2:4–10). St Paul goes even further and tells us that each one of us who form part of the Mystical Body of Christ is a firstborn son and co-heir with Christ (cf. Romans 8:14–17).

So the choice before Israel then, and before us now, is this: Will you be Egypt's slave or the Lord's Anointed? (cf. Hebrews 11:26). God's call gives us a great destiny but we choose to go with God or to stay in Egypt. This choice of ours gives the final direction to our lives.

The heart of the enemy exposed

Pharaoh's response to Moses reveals the heart of the true enemy of God's people (Satan), of whom he was a symbol: 'I will not serve'! He refused Moses' request, saying contemptuously that he did not know the Lord! He was not interested in any new god – Egypt was overflowing with gods. This was the beginning of a long series of refusals to let God come to him with grace and we will see him gradually harden against God.

Pharaoh reflects the attitude of those people who refuse to let God's saving grace operate in their lives. Many want to decide moral issues for themselves and do not recognize the authority of the Church: 'What right has the Church to tell me what to do? I will decide for myself what is good or evil.' This expresses their behaviour. But if they knew the Lord in a personal relationship they would also accept His representation and learn His ways. They would also listen to God's Word and obey it, as Moses and Aaron increasingly did. But to Pharaoh God's Word was only 'glib speeches' (5:9). To the person who refuses to let God into his heart the scriptures (God's words) do not make sense. The Holy Spirit opens them up to the humble and thirsty soul only (cf. 1 Corinthians 2:7–16).

Pharaoh also reflects the evil one in so far as he increased the burdens of the people that very day, accusing them of being lazy (5:8) and having too much time to listen to God's Word coming through Moses and Aaron (v.9). If we remember that 'Faith comes by hearing and hearing from the Word of God' (Romans 10:17), it is easy to see why the evil one wants to keep God's people too busy with work, or with other preoccupations in order to keep them away from the scriptures which would nourish their spiritual life and bring them back to God, causing them to grow (Psalms 19, 119). Pharaoh calls the Word of God 'glib' – empty – speeches; yet why then is he so anxious to keep the people away? It is because he knows that when the Word of God is proclaimed it inflames the people to love and serve God. So we see his dishonesty. It is because the Word of God is powerful and active (Hebrews 12:4) that he fears it and tries to keep God's people away from it.

The increased burdens on the poor slaves open up another important reflection on the work of the devil. When a person is trying to respond to the call of grace in his life, that person often finds that he is surrounded by increased temptation, and increasing demands from those who live and work with him. The enemy uses this device to keep the soul away from hearing the call of grace and responding to it. He tries to discourage the soul in order to make it turn back, so that it will not experience the liberating force of saving grace in his life. Take the alcoholic, for example, who is trying to break away from his bondage, and finds that he is now given many offers of a free drink (just because he has given up alcohol!) and invited to drink parties, whereas in his old drinking days none of these offers were made. Take the person who is trying to turn to God in personal conversion. Before his decision to turn his life over to Christ everything seemed easy, but now he is faced with increased temptations. Add to that increased demands at home or at work and it seems to the poor soul that everything is working to hinder his advancement in holiness. This is the secret influence of the enemy, who operates through people – even good people! – and circumstances to prevent our coming to God. God also works through people and circumstances, trying with His divine grace to draw us into true freedom. So we see that God and the enemy make the same claim on a person, working with the same means. It is the individual person who has the casting vote. He can decide to go with God or

with the devil, just as the Israelites here can decide to go
with Moses or with Pharaoh. Both are making the same
claims on them. Through Moses, God says that Israel is His
firstborn son, and He wants him for Himself – and the devil
says, through Pharaoh, 'These are my slaves and they will
remain at their labours'! (cf. Matthew 11:28–30).

Trouble for Moses (Exodus 5:15–6:1).
Here for the first time we discover that the slaves were not
only building for Pharaoh, but also actually making the
bricks. They were now ordered by Pharaoh to produce the
same number of bricks, but without any straw. It took more
time, and therefore they were harassed by the slave-drivers
(5:13). The foremen of the Israelites were flogged when
they could not produce the daily quota of bricks, and the
slaves were worse placed than they had been before.

The foremen went to Pharaoh to ask him to be
reasonable (vv.15–16), only to be harshly repulsed and
ordered back to work immediately (v.18). As they left
Pharaoh's palace they met Moses and Aaron, who were
waiting for them; the foremen placed the full blame for
their worsened circumstances at Moses' feet (vv. 20–21; cf.
Luke 24:21). Moses' response was to turn to God in prayer.
This was to become the first step in a long life of
intercession for this people (vv. 22–23). After all, he was
only God's representative, so he learned to take his
problems to God, the leader of the people, and let Him
give an answer to their needs (cf. Romans 9:22–24).

Looking at the spiritual message of this sign, we see that
the foremen made a fundamental mistake. Pharaoh
represents the enemy and he is never reasonable! But even
if he did show himself to be reasonable, he is the wrong
master. The Israelites should have turned to their *new
master* in prayer. They should have turned to God. Here
again we see ourselves; God is usually the *last* person we
turn to for help. He is rarely the first! When people are in
distress spiritually they will look for human help – which

is not blameworthy; they may even turn to the enemy for help in spiritualist activities. But how long do they wait before turning to the Lord, our unseen but ever-present friend? God seems to be our last resource, not our first one. The Israelites have to learn that the answer to their terrible plight lies, not with Pharaoh, but with the Lord (cf. Mark 5 for an illustration of this principle). Jesus was the last resort both for Jairus and the woman with the issue of blood. But God waits patiently for us to turn to Him (cf. Isaiah 30:18; Jeremiah 29:11–14).

For Moses this rejection by his own people only confirmed his own doubts about his mission. He had already (4:1) told God that the people might not accept him. This rejection foreshadowed the rejection of Jesus by the Jews. The prophet is not acceptable in his own place or by his own people. Moses' problem was that the situation had got worse, not better! (vv. 22–23). God's response was to reassure his poor servant that the mission would come to a successful conclusion, as he had promised (6:1). But Moses would have to *trust* God and walk in faith (cf. Isaiah 55:11).

The mission re-affirmed (6:2–9)

This second account of Moses' call is a confirmation of his mission in seven powerful promises given by God. Looked at together, they offer great assurance to Moses in his time of trouble. But first God reminded His servant that He is the Covenant God, who always keeps His promises. He reminded Moses also that while He made Himself known to Abraham, and made promises to him in Genesis 17, Abraham never *experienced* God as the Covenant keeper. Abraham and the other patriarchs all died without seeing the fulfilment of the promises (cf. Hebrews 11:13). It was reserved for Moses to experience God as the keeper of His promises. It was through Moses that God would give the Land of Canaan to His chosen people.

God then told Moses that He remembered His Covenant

with Abraham (6:5). This meant that He intended to begin to put the promises into effect.

The seven promises (6:6–8)
These were prefaced by 'I am the Lord':

1. I will free you of the burdens which the Egyptians lay upon you.
2. I will release you from slavery to them.
3. With strokes of power I will deliver you.
4. I will adopt you as my own people.
5. I will be your God.
6. I will bring you to the land I swore that I would give to Abraham, Isaac and Jacob.
7. I will give this land to you for your inheritance.

These seven promises represent the fullness of redemption (Psalm 129), and they pave the way for the incarnation of the Son of God who would fulfil them for all mankind, beyond our greatest expectations, for 'God *wants* to do more for us than we would ever ask or imagine' (Ephesians 3:20). Firstly God promised to release the Israelites from the intolerable burdens placed upon them by their cruel task masters. This reminds us of Jesus' invitation (Matthew 11:28). He also wants to relieve us too from the weight of our own sinfulness and from our broken condition.

But this would not be complete redemption if the people were left as slaves to the wrong master, so redemption involves being bought back – redeemed – from the slave markets of the world and of sin, and being placed under the gentle mastery of the Lord (cf. 1 Peter 1:18f; 1 Corinthians 6:20; Ephesians 1:19).

The redeeming of the Hebrew slaves, and of the slaves of sin, were both accomplished by a mighty intervention of God in history. The Passover was preceded by great acts of power on the part of Moses – the plagues – and the whole miracle ministry of Jesus was His preparation for the fulfilment of Passover on Calvary. In both cases redemption was to be accomplished by the blood of a slain lamb (cf. Exodus 12; 1 Peter 1:18–21).

The fourth promise placed Israel in a unique relationship with God. It put her under God's protection and care in an altogether special way, and prepared her for the uniqueness of the relationship that the people of God would have with Him in the New Testament, where we come to God protected by the New Covenant of Jesus. It makes us His in a very special way, precious to Him.

And it followed then that the Lord would be their God in a rather unique fashion. We will see His intervention on their behalf and what wonderful signs of His love and care he will give them (cf. 2 Corinthians 6:16).

The last two promises gave a homeland to God's redeemed community. They would experience the fulfilment of His promise to Abraham; this would foreshadow the true 'place of rest' (cf. Hebrews 3–4) which God would give His people in the Kingdom of God and afterwards eternally (Ephesians 1:14).

God was speaking like a king. The time had come for Him to show them who He was, and they would see this in the working out of these promises.

God prefaced His seven-fold promise by a declaration of who it was who was making the gift. If we truly know in our experience who He is, then we will experience the enormous assurance that He gives. We can feel secure that He is the one who never breaks His promises (cf. Isaiah 55:1; cf. Luke 1:37).

Moses faithfully related God's promises to Israel, but the people could no longer hear this good news 'so crushed was their spirit and so cruel their slavery' (6:9). They could no longer listen to mere words. Religious theories and doctrines were useless unless backed by action. The spiritual struggle of the people was greater now than before. They had put their trust in God, and in Moses (4:31); with the result that their situation became worse, not better. Their slavery had not crushed their spirit before (1:12), but now they were truly discouraged. This is typical of beginners in the spiritual life. As soon as they turn to God they expect their whole lives to be transformed in a short time, so that when they experience some setback it becomes a major crisis for them, and they are ready to turn away from God again saying, 'It doesn't work! See, I've proved it'! The liberation of the soul is a long, slow process, and patience and perseverance are needed to go through with it step by painful step. We must learn, too, to trust God deeply – not just saying the words 'I trust Him', but learn really to wait on God and let Him work in whatever way and using whatever means He wants. But the poor beginners think this is all too slow; they would rather 'get on with it' and so they will often run ahead of grace, and cause themselves much trouble and disillusionment and discouragement, some of which is not necessary!

This reaction of the people was another problem for an already hesitant Moses, who now turned to God and made his final objection to the mission. 'Look,' said he, 'since the sons of Israel have not listened to me, why should Pharaoh listen to me, a man slow of speech?' (6:12). Reading this makes me wonder whether Moses was not demanding that God should heal his speech impediment! Whatever it was, God had no intention of healing it. He expected Moses to go ahead and accomplish his entire mission with his defect. I think this is worth looking at. None of us like to appear weak, defective or foolish in the eyes of others. Our instinct is to cover up our defects and pretend we are perfect. We demand that imperfections and faults of body as well as character be removed by healing or any other means, so that we can sally forth for God a perfect human being.

But God knows that our faults and defects are good for us, and keep us humble, so he asks us to go forth with our difficulties, but knowing that His grace is sufficient for us and that His power works best through our weakness (2 Corinthians 12:9). It is in the carrying out of the mission that the faults are corrected and the defects healed. And then we can see that whatever good is produced really *is* all God's work, and we are not puffed up with pride. If, when the mission is accomplished, we are still humble, then something very beautiful has happened. We shall see this is Moses' case. Years later, when reflecting on the exodus, the people said that 'Moses was the most humble of men, the humblest man on earth' (Numbers 12:3). So God's refusal to heal him was for a very good purpose. It was the same with St Paul. The 'thorn in his flesh' annoyed him, and he begged God to rid him of it, but God refused and Paul had to continue in the awareness of his weaknesses (2 Corinthians 12:9–10); these very weaknesses made him throw himself on God's mercy and experience God's loving care in a way that would never have happened if he had had no problems. It's not more degrees and diplomas that make us greater servants of God, but a greater degree of humility and trust (cf. Isaiah 40:31).

The work of redemption (7:1–13)

Chapters 1–6 of Exodus set the scene for the great drama of redemption. They introduce us to God's people, God's enemy and God's deliverer, and set the scene for the great event of exodus. Moses' weakness is shown to us very clearly so that we will see redemption as the work of God alone, who condescended to use such a hopeless instrument (1 Corinthians 1:27–31). But from chapter 7 we see a change in Moses. He has finally yielded to God and we will see him grow stronger and stronger as he obeys God's will. His whole glory comes to be in doing God's will; his fame comes from this alone.

Second interview with Pharaoh (7:8–13)

Moses and Aaron went to Pharaoh again to make their request on behalf of the people. Pharaoh demanded a sign from them to show what authority they had for doing this. Moses replied by commanding Aaron to turn his staff into a serpent before them all. Aaron obeyed, but Pharaoh's contemptuous reply was to call his magicians and sorcerers to imitate (and therefore nullify) the sign (cf. Matthew 13:36–43). For a moment if looked as if Moses and Aaron were to fail again, until an unexpected thing happened. Aaron's staff-turned-serpent ate the staffs of the magicians! But even with this turn of events Pharaoh remained stubbornly closed, and the interview finished (cf. 2 Timothy 3:8–9).

What was going on? Again we are faced with the problem of magical trick or God-given sign. First of all, it was normal practice at that time to demand a sign. The Jews were adamant that Jesus produce a sign that they could *understand*, as at Cana of Galilee. It was useless to offer them a sign they could not read. This is important to realize as we read both Exodus and the gospels (Matthew 12:38–42; John 2:11–12). 'This was the first sign of the signs given by Jesus: it was given in Cana of Galilee. He let His glory be seen, and his disciples believed in Him.'

In John 6:30f the Jews demanded a sign greater than the manna in the desert, if Jesus was claiming to be greater than Moses, and therefore the Messiah. Jesus' reply was that He Himself *was*, in His own person, the sign (cf. John 6:50; Luke 2:34). Bread from Heaven. Jesus also offered a sign that would only be seen in His Death and Resurrection (cf. John 1:18–22).

It is interesting that Moses only showed *one* of his signs to Pharaoh. The message of the leprous hand was for God's people needing redemption. It was not for the enemy! But the serpent sign was significant. It could tell Pharaoh and all his people that they were under the influence of the devil – 'the primeval serpent' (Revelation 12:9). It would also show that Moses had power from God to work miracles – just as they said of Jesus: 'Miraculous power is at work in Him' (Mark 6:14).

Pharaoh's response is important. Using the power of the devil, through the occult, he got his magicians to produce more serpents, thus making a bad situation very much worse! The enemy always behaves in this way. We shall see later that Pharaoh did not have the power to reverse the situation, but Moses and Aaron did. Now Aaron's staff ate the other staffs, showing that Moses and Aaron had greater power than did the magicians. They could *remove* the evil and reverse the situation, showing God's saving intention to bring good out of evil. So the hearts of the two opponents are revealed here – God and Satan – and we shall see this principle at work in all the plagues. God's intention is to bring good out of evil, and Satan's intention is to make a bad situation worse.

The conflict just beginning is between the Lord and the Gods of Egypt (cf. Exodus 12:12). In this small contest God has already demonstrated His superior power over the devil. He has declared Himself – through Moses – to be the strong force who intends to invade Satan's kingdom and, having overcome him, set up the Kingdom of God (cf. Luke 10:18–19, 11:21f).

This is shown by the fact that, when the contest is over, Moses and Aaron have removed the staffs from all the magicians and theirs alone remains, and the staff has now become a symbol of their authority to speak and act on behalf of the Lord. They use this staff for all of God's work from now on.

But we should not underestimate the power of the evil one either. He too is able to empower his followers to work miracles. People today like to brush aside any talk of the occult because they are afraid to face the very real spiritual conflict that is being waged in our world. If we do face what is happening and throw our weight on the side of Christ, we can be part of the answer to evil, but if we close our eyes to the presence of the enemy he will have freedom to work. We can stand up to him and conquer him as Moses and Aaron did in the exodus, and as the early Church did in the Roman Empire (cf. 1 Peter 5:9–11). As servants of God we must go forth in the power of God to conquer the enemy, otherwise it will be the 'prince of this world' who will rule our planet, and not Christ, and the fault will be ours.

In this conflict we will see Moses oppose the magicians

until he overcomes them (2 Timothy 3:8). In the first challenge he has already removed their symbol of authority – the staff – and by the third plague they are put out of action (8:14–15, 18–19). They end up acknowledging that Moses' miracles show the 'finger of God' (Luke 11:20), i.e. they acknowledge the Lord's power and presence and bow out of the contest. Their final humiliation will come when they are covered with boils and unable even to face Moses (9:11).

The Plagues (chapters 7-11)
As we approach chapter 7, we almost feel an impatience to see some action! An impatience to see what is to come.

We now move into open warfare between God and Pharaoh. It began with a sign of death – the waters of the Nile turned to blood – but it was to end with the reality, the death of the firstborn of all Egypt. God was about to show His power and manifest His wonders to all Egypt (3:20). It is very important to see that this struggle is between God and the *gods* of Egypt (12:12). It will become clear as we go through these events that the number and severity of the plagues depended absolutely on Pharaoh. The plagues would stop the moment he bent his stubborn heart to the Lord, but if he persisted in his obstinacy – as he did – God would make each plague more severe than the last one, until He had brought Egypt to the brink of ruin (10:7), and this ruler, this prodigal son, to his knees (10:16–17; Luke 15).

But we shall see that, no matter what happened or how great the price that had to be paid, Pharaoh would refuse to submit to God: he fought God to the very end, and died in his obduracy. No wonder he is such a good symbol of that angel of light who was thrown out of Heaven for his defiant refusal to serve God! (Revelation 12:7–9).

There were ten plagues altogether:

1. The water of the Nile was turned to blood (7:14–25).

2. Frogs covered the land (7:26–8:15).
3. Lice (mosquitoes) attacked their bodies (8:16–19).
4. Gadflies invaded the land (8:20–32).
5. The Egyptians' cattle died (9:1–7).
6. Boils attacked the Egyptians (9:8–12).
7. Hailstorms brought destruction (9:13–35).
8. Locusts destroyed the harvest (10:1–20).
9. There was total darkness for the Egyptians only (10:21–29).
10. The firstborn of Egypt died (11:1–10, 12:29–34).

In 7:4 these plagues are called either 'acts of power' or acts of judgement. They constitute 'the signs and wonders' that God had promised to perform (7:3, 8:23, 10:1f, 11:9f; and cf. Deuteronomy, 6:20–25, 26:5–11; Psalm 78:44–51, 125:28–36).

Did the plagues actually happen? We moderns continuously stumble over the question of historicity in the Bible. The question 'did it actually happen?' is quickly followed by 'when and how did it happen?' When we do not find satisfactory answers to these questions we cast doubt on the truth of scripture itself.

First: the ancients did not handle historical facts in the way that we do. Our demand for scientific accuracy regarding events, names, places and dates would leave them uninterested. They asked – and expect us who read their works to ask – 'What does it mean?' They wanted an interpretation of events rather than an accurate listing of them, so we search in vain for accuracy of detail according to *our* definition of 'fact'.

The biblical authors wrote religious history; they present all happenings from the standpoint of what it means through the eyes of faith. It is an interpretation of history that they have left to us rather than the dry bones of 'what happened'. When we read of the plagues within the context of the exodus we see the theological interpretation of God's most famous intervention in the history of man before the coming of Christ.

Interpreters of the Bible tell us that there was a natural cause for most of the plagues. For example, the annual flooding of the Nile brought a brownish mass of red earth mixed with algae with it, which had a foul smell. And the increase of frogs after the flooding of the Nile is well known. Lice, flies and mosquitoes would find a natural breeding ground in small pools of water containing decaying frogs. The retreat of the foul-smelling Nile, after its flooding, gave rise to illness among cattle. Plagues of cattle disease were known in Egypt as recently as 1842, 1863 and 1866. The boils could also be traced to the Nile and the frogs as the source of the trouble. As regards the hail, powerful thunderstorms are normal at certain times of the year. Plagues of locusts are well known all over the Middle East. As for the darkness, there is a dust storm known as *Khamsa* where fine particles drift with the wind. It can be denser than fog – so thick it can be *felt*.[1]

The plagues of Egypt are not given to us as *unnatural* events, events that could not or did not happen before. They are interventions by God in the history of man in a world made by Him. He created the universe and acts through it. He is the author of what we call 'Nature'. He spoke to His people through 'natural' events – such as the frogs, flies, disease of cattle, locusts, hailstorms, etc. It is what God is saying *through* these events that constitutes the message of scripture. The hailstorm in itself may be a natural event – part of God's ordinary everyday dealing with us – but the power Moses had to bring it on and to stop it through prayer was neither 'natural' or usual!

Why would God choose – out of all possible ways of communication – to speak to Egypt through these particular signs? Firstly, God had to speak to the Egyptians through signs that they would understand if communication was to be established. So we ask: did frogs and lice carry a message for Egypt which is now lost or

---

[1] cf. *Plagues of Egypt* by Greta Hurst, footnotes to *His Way Out*, pp. 70–71.

unknown to most of us? I think yes! Egypt represented a very ancient civilization which worshipped a whole pantheon of gods. There was a god for everything from earth to sky, every event of life came under the power and jurisdiction of some deity, thus making life very complex indeed.

In this contest the Lord was taking on the gods of Egypt (12:12), and He had to demonstrate their powerlessness to protect the people from the only real God – the Lord, the Living God. In the early days of the Church's missionary work St Paul met a similar problem in Athens (cf. Acts 17). The people of Athens even had a statue erected to 'the unknown God' to make sure no deity was excluded from their worship!

Another very real problem here is that Pharaoh himself was worshipped as a divine person and was surrounded by a whole pagan priesthood which kept him in that illusion; he would not be open to acknowledging someone greater than himself. So the plagues of Egypt were aimed at Pharaoh and his whole pantheon of gods.[2] Different names and functions have been suggested for the gods of Egypt. The following is a summary of some of these suggestions as they relate to the plagues: The Nile was worshipped as a god, the source of life. The frog represented the god Heka or Heket. Lice would insult Seth, the god of the earth. The flies would represent Beelzebub, the Lord of the Flies (cf. Matthew 12:24, note f, Jerusalem Bible) and the prince of devils. But some say that the flies aimed at the god Kephra. The lice and the flies, therefore, attacked all idolatrous worship and worshippers; cleanliness was an imperative element of Egyptian worship; the priests wore white linen next to their skin and shaved their bodies every day.[3]

Cattle and horses were considered sacred animals.

[2] cf. L. Grollenberg, O.P., in *Atlas of the Bible*, shows a photo of a statue of Pharaoh as a god with the symbol of the snake in his crown.
[3] cf. *Companion Bible*, p. 84.

Ashes were used to bless the people; so in the fifth plague the 'blessing' was turned into a curse. Some say that this sixth plague was aimed at Neit, the mother goddess of heaven, but others say that it was aimed at Typhon (the evil principle).[4] The seventh plague showed that Isis and Osiris, the gods of fire and water, were powerless before the hailstorm. The god Seraphis was supposed to protect the land from locusts but failed in the eighth plague. The ninth plague showed that Ra, the sun god, and Set, the god of evil, had no power before the Lord, the Light of the World. Pharaoh himself was brought down by the tenth plague, which showed that neither he nor his heir had any power over death.[5]

When the contest between Pharaoh and God was over, the Lord had shown everyone that He alone deserved the Name of God, and that He alone could protect His people. This He demonstrated from the fourth plague; from that point onwards we see that the Israelites were spared (8:16; 9:4; 10:23; 11:7) and only those opposing God were afflicted.

Pharaoh had discovered that he was *not* divine and had even acknowledged his guilt before God (10:16). St Paul later spoke of the triumph of Christ in words that would explain God's triumph here (Colossians 2:15).

The purpose of the plagues

They had a twofold purpose. Firstly, they were a demonstration for Egypt and the 'world'. Secondly, they were for Israel and believers. To Egypt and the world, God wanted to demonstrate His power and His presence (8:19; 9:16) and bring judgement on Pharaoh and on Egypt for enslaving Israel. It was judgement for all gods of Egypt, too. The plagues were to demonstrate that the Lord is the only God (18:11), greater than all gods, and at the same

[4] cf. *Companion Bible*.
[5] Following suggestions by B. L. Ramm, *His Way Out*, p. 61.

time to show up the depravity of unregenerate man in clear and precise terms, therefore showing up our need for Redemption.

The plan of the plagues

The plagues follow a particular pattern. They are given in three sets of three as a preparation for the tenth and final stroke of God. In each of the three sets a warning is given for the first and second plague, but the third is given without warning and seems to be a real punishment. There is also a progressive plan in them, beginning with a warning of death in plague 1 but followed by actual death of the firstborn in plague 10; a warning about darkness in plague 2 followed by real darkness in plague 9. The magicians recognize God's hand in plague, but Pharaoh waits until plague 8; plagues 4 and 5 show God discriminating in favour of Israel. Plague 6 stands alone.

The moral message of the plagues

PLAGUE 1: THE NILE – BLOOD: 'The wages of sin is death' (Romans 6:23). The world of unregenerate man is self-destructive in its ways. These ways not only lead to the human disasters in which history abounds, but also to the loss of God which is *real* death.

PLAGUE 2: Frogs are creatures of night and so speak of the spiritual darkness hovering over such a world – a darkness made dense by pride. (Cf. Revelation 16:13f).

PLAGUE 3: The lice or mosquitoes: 'dust thou art and unto dust thou shalt return' (Genesis 3:19). This speaks of the spiritual impurity and uncleanness of a world given over to immorality (Romans 1–3).

PLAGUE 4: Gadflies remind us of Beelzebub – the Lord of the Flies – which is one of the titles for the devil (Matthew 12:24). This would point to the devil being the real power behind a world system dominated by idolatry, immorality, darkness and pride (plagues 1–4).

PLAGUE 5: Cattle are beasts of burden and point to the burdens of spiritual slavery.

PLAGUE 6: Boils (cf. Isaiah 1:2–6). People living the type of life described in plagues 1–6 are sick in God's eyes and need healing.

PLAGUE 7: The hail shows us God's judgement on disobedience and obstinacy.

PLAGUE 8: The locusts leave a country barren and so represent the soul before God – barren and without spiritual fruit.

PLAGUE 9: The person who lives by this world system is in spiritual darkness leading to

PLAGUE 10: Spiritual death (Hell).

Put together, the message of plagues 1–10 is that the world desperately needs the Lord to come and save it! If God did not present us with true self-knowledge we would never turn to Him for help. We would stay in our pride and darkness (plagues 2 and 9), a burden to ourselves and others (plague 5), weighted down by our own sins (plague 6), persisting in self will (plague 7), utterly useless and barren (plague 8), in darkness and spiritual blindness (plague 9). It is essential that God tells us our sins and so gives us a chance to repent.

> Yet you are merciful to all, because you can do all things and overlook men's sins so that they can repent – you spare all things because all things are yours, Lord, lover of life, you whose imperishable spirit is in all. Little by little, therefore, you correct those who offend, you admonish and remind them of how they have sinned, so that they may abstain from evil and trust in you, Lord.
>
> (Wisdom 11:24, 12:1–2)

(See also Psalms 50 and 51.) John the Baptist, following the practice of all the prophets before him, found it necessary to tell Israel her sins before the coming of Jesus so that she would know her need for redemption (cf. Matthew 3:1–2; Luke 3:1–18).

The plagues as a message for Israel

The same plagues that spoke such an urgent message of the
need for repentance to Egypt contained another message
for the poor Hebrew slaves: they were living in a country
given over to idolatry whose priests (the magicians) could
produce miracle signs. The Lord showed them that *He*
could perform *greater* signs. Therefore He is the God of all
gods (cf. Psalm 86:10; Isaiah 37:16, 44:8, 45:22).

The plagues were meant to build up the Hebrews' faith
and trust in God, who would do such wonderful things to
save them. They saw the Lord as Sovereign Lord of the
Universe, the One with absolute control, and this great
Lord was present and fighting their battles for them. So
God demonstrates clearly that even though He was unseen
He was very much present, and was always on the side of
the oppressed (Psalm 34:18); as He brought down all the
gods of Egypt they knew that He was the only, true living
God.

The first plague (7:14–25)

The Lord told Moses that Pharaoh was adamant and that
he was to go ahead with the first sign (v.14). Moses was to
meet Pharaoh on his way to the river Nile (for his morning
bath?) the following day (v.15) and tell him that it was
because he had not listened to God (v.16) that Moses was
going to perform this miracle, using his staff (cf. 4:1–6).
The water would turn into blood and the fish in the river
would die; this would make a foul smell so that the
Egyptians would not want to drink from the Nile (vv.17–
18). The sign was given and the water of the river changed
into blood. Pharaoh was not impressed because his
magicians were able through their witchcraft to repeat the
same sign. They made matters worse – whatever water was
left after Moses and Aaron gave their sign was now turned
into blood. Pharaoh just walked away in disdain (v.23),

apparently not caring about the hardship to his people, and this awful situation lasted for seven days! His lack of compassion for his *own* people, not to speak of the Hebrews, shows up the evil heart of this man. Contrast this with the descriptions of a compassionate God in the New Testament (cf. Matthew 9:26, 14:14; Luke 10:33, 15:20).

This first sign given by Moses stands out in awful contrast to the first sign given by Jesus in the New Testament. Water is a symbol of the Word of God and of the grace of God (John 4, and 7; Isaiah 12; John 15:3; Ephesians 5:26). Moses declared in this sign that finally to reject God's Word and God's grace, freely given to us, would lead to real death (Hell). It was a serious warning to the sinful world, which wants to go its own way without God, and without obedience to His Word. The prophets after Moses, and John the Baptist too, were equally strong in warning the people of the dire consequences of rejecting God's Word and His invitation to save us (cf. Matthew 3:8–10; Mark 16:16; Jeremiah 44:20–28; Amos 4:4–12).

But Jesus' first sign was to change water into wine! Good news indeed: 'the law was given by Moses but grace and truth came in Jesus Christ' (John 1:17). The law – which Moses was called to give – could only point out evil and its consequences. It could not cure the evil. This is illustrated in the parable of the Good Samaritan, when the priest and the Levite walked past the oppressed man; they could *do* nothing about his condition. It was only Jesus, the Saviour, the Good Samaritan, who could heal the man's wounds and set him on the way to eternal life. Jesus came to re-create heaven in the human heart; to heal and restore all that had been destroyed by sin – to change the water of our lives into the wine of God's love.

Under Moses and the mosaic law sinners would tremble, but under Jesus sinners could rejoice in the forgiving, healing love of God.

The second plague (7:26–8:11)

Seven days had passed since the first sign was given. The number seven can represent a perfect completed work, here it represents the fact that God gave Pharaoh plenty of time to think things over and to repent, thus showing God's patience (Romans 9:22–23).

But Pharaoh did not repent, and Moses had to go to him to perform his second sign. Again Moses requested permission to take the Hebrews to offer worship to the Lord; if Pharaoh refused, the whole country would be plagued by frogs. Now frogs are harmless creatures, but nobody wants them all over his house and food! There is a real touch of humour here as Moses told Pharaoh that the frogs would even make their way into the palace, and into the king's bedroom . . . and bed . . . and into his ovens and kneading bowls! There would be no escape from these ubiquitous frogs! Again the Lord commanded Moses to get Aaron to use the staff of God to work this wonder (7:28 or 8:3).

The magicians repeated the sign and so the country was doubly dosed with frogs. The magicians had, again, made the situation worse (8:3). But we make an interesting discovery at this point. The magicians could bring on the plague but they could not remove it. Pharaoh knew that only Moses and Aaron could remove the scourge; he had learnt this lesson in the second interview when Aaron's staff had swallowed the magicians' staffs (7:8–13).

There is another extraordinary element introduced into the narrative at this point also, and that is that Pharaoh felt free to turn to Moses, whom he opposed so much – and ask him to pray to the Lord to remove the plague (8:4). Respect for Moses was growing already.

It says a lot for Moses that he was prepared to comply with such a request. If Moses had *wanted* the Egyptians to suffer, he could have refused, but it is obvious from Moses' behaviour in all the plagues, that neither he nor the Lord wanted the people to suffer; the plague would be removed at the first sign of repentance, even when it was not permanent repentance.

Moses was also growing in stature as a man of God. We see him here manifesting a much greater confidence in God than before. He said to Pharaoh 'What time am I to fix for the frogs to leave you and your subjects?' (8:5). Moses was sure that he was doing God's will and that God would respond favourably to his intercession – even on behalf of his enemy! 'Pray for those who persecute you . . .' (Matthew 5:44). Moses reminded Pharaoh that if the Lord did remove the scourge, Pharaoh had to learn from it. God was not working these signs for nothing! There was a message both in the appearance and in the removal of the plagues. If the plague was removed at Moses' request, then Pharaoh was to learn that the Lord had no equal (8:6). Pharaoh was being asked to recognize the Lord as the only true god.

Moses prayed and God heard his prayer. The frogs all died and were piled up in heaps until the country reeked with their decaying carcases (vv. 8–10). But now the heart of Pharaoh is revealed; as soon as the plague was removed he went back to his old position of stubborn refusal. So, if the purpose of the second plague had been to bring Pharaoh to repentance, it was a failure.

The third plague (8:12–15)

This third sign formed the first real punishment. It was given without warning but by now the sign could be understood. Moses was instructed by God to command Aaron to strike the ground with his staff, and the very dust of the earth would rise up and afflict all living things, both man and beast. No one would escape. Moses obeyed, and the lice attacked everyone. The magicians tried but failed to reproduce this sign, and in their failure they recognized that Moses had power superior to theirs. They went to Pharaoh and declared that this sign was 'the finger of God' manifested to them (8:19).

To see why this sign was so special, why the presence and intervention of God was recognized by the magicians, we need to go back to Genesis where God declared that the ground was accursed because of the sin of mankind: 'Accursed be the soil because of you . . . for dust you are and unto dust you shall return' (Genesis 3:17,19).

This sign was aimed at the pride of man telling us that we were made from the dust of the earth; what right have we to rebel against Him who made us and who sustains life in us, He who cares for us and wants to save us? (Romans 9:14–24). The magicians realized that this sign was the finger of God writing in the dust of the earth to convict His people of their sin. Jesus performed a similar action for the leaders of Israel in His own day, when they brought to Him for judgement a woman who had committed adultery. The message Jesus wrote with His finger in the dust convinced *them* of sin, and 'they all moved away beginning with the eldest' (cf. John 8:6–10). Jesus also declared to the Jewish leaders that He performed His miracles by the finger of God. In this way He claimed that His work manifested God's presence and power among them (cf. Luke 11:20). But it was often only the demon spirits in possessed people who recognized this presence and power in Jesus, while the obstinate and blind saw nothing. We see this here with Pharaoh also. The sign means nothing to him, or he is not open to learn from it (8:15 (19); cf. Mark 5:7–10).

The fourth plague (8:16–28)
This is the first of the second series of plagues. The second three were to be more severe than the first. In the first round of this contest the people were disturbed and annoyed by the blood, frogs and lice, but in this second round they were to experience the destruction of their harvest and their livestock. God moved in on their possessions and then even on their own persons, with the plague of boils.

A new element is brought in at this stage: God made a distinction between Egypt and Israel. From now on the people in the land of Goshen would be spared from the

80

plagues. This action of God the Bible calls 'putting redemption between them'. It meant that those choosing to co-operate with redemption went over to God's side of the battle line and only those resisting God's action experienced the plagues. God calls those who accept redemption 'my people' (v.19), and all those who refuse it 'your people', i.e. people of the world. Jesus did the same in John's gospel (8:44–47).

We are told that the gadflies 'ruined the country' (v.20). Pharaoh sent for Moses, and began to negotiate with him at last. 'Go and offer sacrifice to your God *but in this country*' (v.22). The king grudgingly admitted that the Lord *is* a God to be worshipped, but he did not want the Israelites to leave Egypt. The contradiction in his behaviour is obvious. At first he had wanted to kill off the children (1:16) in order to destroy the race; now he does not want any of them to go because they are useful to him.

In the negotiations which begin now there are two interesting things to notice. 1. Pharaoh continues to try to CHANGE God's Word to Moses, since he could no longer nullify it with his magicians. 2. Moses holds out tenaciously for what God had demanded; in the end he gets everything he asks for.

This struggle shows up the work of the enemy again, who hates God's Word and who, from the beginning, tried to change it. He said to the unsuspecting Eve, 'Did God *really* say . . .?' thus sowing doubt in her heart. Eve answered him truthfully as to what God had commanded, then the serpent contradicted God's Word, 'No! you will not die!' . . . but she *did* die and with her all mankind! (Genesis 3). Jesus told us that we must become as wise as the serpent (Matthew 10:16) and thus fight the enemy with his own weapons. It is God's Word pure and undefiled that we must hold on to and live out; then we too, like Moses and all the servants of God after him, will experience in our own lives the fulfilment of all that God has promised. 'God is truth; in Him there is no lie' (cf. 2 Corinthians 2:11).

This was God's message to Moses:

1. He was to request a three-days' journey into the wilderness to offer sacrifice to God (3:18).
2. The Israelites were to keep a feast for God in the wilderness (5:1).
3. As God's firstborn son among the nations, Israel was being called to serve God (4:23).
4. Before they left, His people were to take jewellery and other valuables – which obviously they would need for bartering (3:21–22).
5. God would be waiting for them on the mountain (Sinai or Horeb) (3:12).

The order of the requests is important. The Israelites were to offer sacrifice to God first and *then* keep a feast for Him in the wilderness, after which they would become His sons and serve Him, and He would consecrate them to Him as His own people on the mountain.

This is the correct order of things in the redemptive process. Jesus had to be sacrificed on Calvary to take away our sins and atone for all the accumulated guilt of man, *before* we, as His new people of God, could celebrate the feast and become His holy people consecrated to Him and His service (1 Corinthians 5:8; Acts 27:23). In order to celebrate our new life in Christ, Paul tells us that we must get rid of the old life of sin and wickedness. For Moses and the Hebrews that meant *leaving* Egypt and all it stood for. We *all* have to leave 'Egypt' before we can begin our heavenly life in Christ (Colossians 1:1–3).

Let us now look at Pharaoh, representing as he does 'the god of this world' (John 14:30). We first had his stubborn refusal 'I will *not* let Israel go'! But after three plagues that finally put his magicians out of action, and a fourth one which only affected him and his people, he had to give a little, even if grudgingly. But there was no question of him allowing Israel to leave Egypt altogether – he wanted to keep them under his power. But Moses would not accept this change in God's plan. They were to make a three-day journey *into the wilderness* (v. 24) and that meant leaving Egypt. Pharaoh conceded on condition they did not go too far away (v.25). He is lengthening the chain, but it is still a chain. He even requested them to pray for him – their persecutor! There is subtlety at work here. Pharaoh is saying, 'Be reasonable, if you have to worship your god, do it openly here in Egypt like everyone else. There is no need for this big procession to the wilderness. Then everyone will see how accommodating I am to let even my slaves worship their strange God!'

Through Pharaoh the scriptures again teach us about the subtle wiles of the enemy, who at all costs does not want us to experience our freedom as the sons of God (cf. Romans 8:14–17), nor to become a free, worshipping community with the Lord as our centre. If he cannot have us completely enslaved then he tries to keep us miserable, not fully experiencing our freedom in Christ. This hatred of his is seen in the hatred of 'the world' for God's people (cf. John 15:19, 17:14), and its continual persecution of the Church all down the centuries.

In order to experience our full glory as Sons of God we must break away totally from 'the snare of the fowler who seeks to destroy us' (Psalm 90:3), from the enslaving influences of the unbelieving world, *and* from self, in order to cling to the Lord. Only then will we understand and want to sing the song of deliverance:

> When the Lord delivered Sion from bondage
>   it seemed like a dream
> Then was our mouth filled with laughter
>   on our lips there were songs.
>
> Even the heathen said 'What marvels
>   the Lord worked for them!'
> What marvels the Lord worked for us
>   indeed we were glad!

(Psalm 126:1–2)

It is going to mean everything to Moses and to us – to hold out tenaciously against all the wiles of the enemy, in order that we can rejoice in our full liberation and go on to experience the union with God to which the Lord calls us. The enemy lost his position in Heaven and is determined that we will never find ours (John 14:2; Revelation 12:7–9). It is important for us to recognize how he works and to stand up to him with strong faith and trust in God until we overcome him (cf. James 4:8; 1 Peter 5:6–10). Jesus gave His life in order that we would experience our full life in Christ. Let us not settle for less (John 10:10).

The voice of the devil and the world sounds so reasonable: 'Avoid extremes; don't be fanatical; be sensible about your spiritual life; there is no need to be "different" or narrow-minded' . . . this voice is the same for us today. If we hold back because of public opinion we will never reach union with God, and we will never become completely happy or fulfilled.

Jesus (our Moses) calls us out from 'the world'. This means that he wants us freed from its low moral standards; we should behave like children in God's family, guided by His Word and empowered by His grace, led by His Spirit. We are to remain in the world but not 'of it' (John 17:15), we are to live by the principles of the Kingdom of God (Colossians 3:1; Hebrews 3:1). To live like this is noticeably different from the evil ways of the world (1 John 2:6). But it is not difficult because 'in His presence is fullness of joy' (Psalm 16:11).

Moses has come to know Pharaoh now and is not impressed, and warns him not to go back on his word again (v.26). We see here that God is using Moses to show this proud king that he is not only human but sinful. Pharaoh must accept this in his heart if he is to acknowledge God as the Lord.

The expected happened! The pattern is the same in each stage of the conflict. Moses prayed – the plague was removed by God through Moses' intercession and, as soon as the trouble stopped, Pharaoh fell back into his old stubborn ways – thus forcing God to reveal His hand even more strongly than before!

The fifth plague (9:1–7)

Moses was again ordered to go before the King and request that God's people could go and worship Him (vv.1,2). If Pharaoh refused then only the cattle of the Egyptians would die – God would spare the cattle of Israel to show His presence and power. This was a greater sign than if all the livestock were to be stricken indiscriminately, because it would be difficult to explain the protection of the livestock of Israel (v.4). Pharaoh was impressed; made enquiries and found the facts to be exactly as Moses had said! (v.7). But he would not repent. He stayed as obdurate as ever, thus forcing God to act again.

The sixth plague (9:8–12)

Moses was told to take handfuls of ashes or soot from 'the kiln' and throw them in the air in front of Pharaoh (v.9). The ashes would become fine dust spreading all over Egypt and producing boils on animals as well as man (v.10). The magicians were also attacked by them and could no longer even face Moses! They were finally defeated (v.11). But Pharaoh was as untouched by this as by any other sign. The ashes used for this sign came from the kiln beside Pharaoh's palace. It was not any ordinary furnace that we are dealing with here, but one of the altars on which human sacrifices were made to the god Typhon.

So, what we see here is that the Lord took the results of their pagan worship and threw it in Pharaoh's face to show him what God thought of it![1] Human sacrifice was not acceptable to the Lord and did not make man acceptable in His sight. This type of worship showed that mankind was sick in God's eyes (cf. Isaiah 1:4–6).

[1] cf. *Companion Bible*, p. 85.

The seventh plague (9:13–35)

This is the first of the third series of plagues. God knew that Pharaoh would never give in, so He decided to unleash the rest of His signs on him (v.14). The proud king would be forced to acknowledge God as the Sovereign Lord of the Universe (v.14). God goes even further and explains why He did not just annihilate Pharaoh; why He has shown patience towards him, allowing Himself to be pushed to show greater and greater signs. The reason was that God can use even the sinfulness of man to manifest His glory (v.16) on the earth. The people at that time would not understand a God who showed mercy and patience with His people! No, their whole need in worship was to placate the anger of their many deities. So, through Pharaoh's sinfulness the people began to see the nature and character of the Lord, the True God, who would defend a band of slaves against the most powerful king on earth. He must be a great God indeed! And He must be loving – to fight their battles for them like this.

God manifested His humility in even entering into dialogue with such a perverse man as Pharaoh. He also showed that he prefers to work through people as His representatives, and that His words would be more clearly understood coming from the mouths of weak human beings like Moses and Aaron.

Jesus followed this pattern also in promising that His disciples would do even greater works than He Himself did, when he had gone back to the Father (John 14:12). God works quietly and unobtrusively through those people who are open to Him and willing to serve others. It is beautiful to see the amazement of the disciples when they discover for the first time in their own experience that Jesus really *has* given them the power to heal and work wonders (Luke 10:17–20).

God would use us also, in whatever situation of life we find ourselves, if only we too are open to his purpose and care enough about the plight of suffering humanity to want to do something about it. But we make excuses; we say that it was all right for them; they were great people *anyway*. But the scriptures show us otherwise. Neither Moses nor the Apostles were anything before they met the Living God in the Lord and Jesus. It was in his relationship with God that Moses *became* great and famous and was motivated to do great things for Israel. It was exactly the same with the Apostles and will be with us; when we enter into a deeply fulfilling and life-giving relationship with Jesus we, too, will find the love of God urging us to do great things to serve our neighbour.

A new element comes into the plagues at this point. The Egyptians are told that if any of them obey the Lord from now on He will spare them as well as Israel. If they bring their animals and slaves in from the fields and put them under cover they will be spared from the hail (v.19). Some of them did obey, out of fear of the Lord. The king's courtiers no longer obeyed their earthly king – but the One who was manifesting His presence so powerfully. They had all been dealing with Moses long enough to know that his word was law (cf. Acts 4:19).

It is interesting also to observe the Lord appealing to the people over Pharaoh's head. God was claiming to be the universal king and demanding obedience from His subjects in the world.

Fear is often the first step in our journey to God – fear of punishment, as we observe here. But scripture tells us that 'the fear of the Lord is the *beginning* of wisdom' (cf. Psalm 111:10). When we enter into relationship with God we discover the wonderful qualities in Him that drive out that fear (as the Israelite slaves were now discovering them). Fear remained a part of Israel's relationship to the Lord throughout her history. It was not until Jesus came, manifesting the heart of God as the compassionate and merciful Father of all, that 'perfect love could cast out all fear' (cf. Luke 15; 1 John 4:18).

The tragedy is that today many people still relate to God

87

in fear, as if God had never shown His heart to us in Jesus and the Holy Spirit. They still feel that he is the avenger, and so keep His laws in order to avoid punishment. The solution to this problem is simple but profound. We must ask Jesus in prayer to manifest Himself and the Father to us personally so that we can grow in our relationship with Them (John 14:21). Then we commit our lives to Him and His service, and enter into a life-giving relationship with Him that will be our happiness and fulfilment even in this life.

The plague of hail was very severe (v.18), damaging crops and vegetation throughout Egypt. But the Land of Goshen had no hail, thus showing again that the Lord discriminated (or put redemption) between Israel and Egypt. Anyone siding with the Lord was protected now, which meant that he had gone over to the side of redemption and come under God's rule and protection.

Pharaoh was distressed enough to send for Moses and Aaron and actually admit that he had sinned, that the Lord was right and that his stubborn refusal to obey was wrong! (v.27). But there is repentance and repentance, and Moses knew Pharaoh well enough now to realize that a *real* change of heart (which is the meaning of repentance) had not yet happened! (v.30). And when God removed the plague at Moses' request 'Pharaoh sinned yet again' (9:35). What was wrong with Pharaoh was that he feared the thunderstorm but what he *needed* was fear of the Lord!

God expected Pharaoh and his subjects to learn the lesson of this plague and acknowledge His sovereignty over the earth (v.30).

The eighth plague (10:1–20)

Moses was now sent to Pharaoh to demand why he had not yet submitted to the Lord; we see again that if this proud and arrogant king had only submitted to Him the plagues would have been averted (v.3). When Moses announced the plague of locusts (vv. 4–6) it was the last straw for the courtiers. They could no longer stand aside waiting for Pharaoh's orders, they urged him to let the people go, because Egypt was 'on the brink of ruin' (v.7).

Pharaoh compromised again. He would let the men go (v.11) but hold on to the children as hostages to force the men to come back! But Moses held out for the full request of the Lord – i.e. that the whole nation of Israel should move out, with all their possessions and livestock. It was now clear to Pharaoh and everyone involved that they would not be coming back (vv.9–10). Why would they want to go back to Egypt after all they had experienced there? They would feel as the Apostles did when Jesus challenged them as to whether *they* wanted to go back to their old way of life, 'Lord, to whom would we go? You alone have the words of eternal life' (John 6:67–69).

Anyone who has ever been in the Middle East or Africa would know how terrifying a plague of locusts is! They eat up all the green vegetation in sight and reduce the country to a barren wasteland in a short time. The harvest is destroyed in a few short hours, bringing famine in its wake (vv. 14,15). It even terrified the mighty king of Egypt! He sent urgently for Moses and Aaron, admitted openly for the first time that he had sinned, both against the Lord and against Moses and Aaron! He begged both forgiveness and the removal of this deadly plague (vv.16,17). Pharaoh looks really repentant here, but he is not. He is only afraid of the consequences of the plague. As soon as relief comes he will go back to resisting God, as he has been doing all along (v.20).

There must have been a relationship of mutual respect

between Pharaoh and Moses. They had come to know each other very well. The ease with which the king asked, and expected to receive, forgiveness from Moses is lovely to see. The holiness of Moses shines out each time he grants forgiveness to this stubborn man, continually prays on his behalf . . . and makes requests to God for him! If Moses were not the true man of God that he had become he would have behaved with anger and revenge towards the Pharaoh, because he had real power at his disposal. But, like Jesus later, he would not use this power for his own benefit. He was truly serving God and his neighbour (cf. Matthew 4:4–11). His unworldly approach shows up his deep relationship with God.

Before we leave this plague it would be good to contrast Pharaoh with the image of the Prodigal Son in Luke 15. I wonder if Jesus had this incident in mind as he put Pharaoh's words into the mouth of the prodigal son when he returned to his father? 'I have sinned against heaven and before you. I am not worthy to be called your son' (Luke 15:18–19). There is a clear teaching on sin given in both of these texts. Pharaoh's resistance to God's call and God's grace had brought Egypt to the brink of economic ruin. The parable of the prodigal son shows us that the boy's sin brought disgrace to his family and disaster upon himself. In both cases we are told clearly that it is not possible to sin 'against Heaven' alone! Sin always affects our neighbour and brings misery and disaster in its train. Even such a basic sin as selfishness brings a great deal of unhappiness to the home or community in which we live. The misery and disgrace to the family or community of the alcoholic or drug addict is proverbial.

From this we see that our repentance will also affect our neighbour. True change of heart affects not only our relationship with God, but also all those we live with. If Pharaoh repented here all Egypt would benefit from it! We need to be more aware of our responsibility towards others. We can *decide* to be a source of happiness or pain depending on our attitudes and behaviour.

The ninth plague (10:21–29)

This ninth plague came as the third punishment without warning (the others were numbers 3 and 6). Moses stretched out his hand towards Heaven, and Egypt was plunged into a terrifying three days of total darkness. This darkness was not just the absence of light, which could have been overcome by the use of torches. No. It was a darkness so 'thick that it could be felt'! No one could either see or move about for three days (v.23). This brought the country to a complete stop. But the message of the sign was even greater than this: the land of Goshen had light! The Israelites were spared yet again.

Pharaoh was impressed. It was unheard of to have both light and darkness in the land at the same time. This Lord was great indeed! Pharaoh summoned Moses and gave permission for all the Israelites to go and worship the Lord, but they were to leave their livestock behind (v.24). It is obvious that without the flocks and herds the people could neither worship the Lord nor survive! To worship the Lord they would have to sacrifice some of the animals, and the animals they sacrificed were sacred to the Egyptians, like sheep and cattle; it is clear that Pharaoh wanted to confiscate the flocks and herds for himself after all the destruction of the plagues (vv.25,26). So they ended up in deadlock once again.

The sign-message in this ninth plague is very powerful. 'God is Light; there is no darkness in Him at all' (1 John 1:15). Darkness is the absence or *withdrawal* of light. The absence of light speaks of the kingdom of darkness and of Satan. The withdrawal of light speaks of God's punishment for sin. People who drive God out of their lives find themselves lost in darkness (cf. 1 John 1:5–7). Three days of darkness would denote God's full withdrawal from Egypt. This means the removal of His protecting hand; thus the Egyptians would be exposed to the angel of death in the tenth plague. The Israelites, on the other hand, had light and were therefore protected by God's plan of redemption, so that the angel of death would pass over them (as in the passover) and they would live. This *is* redemption.

Egypt was being told in this sign that she had chosen darkness rather than light. She had rejected God, and so God had withdrawn Himself – had abandoned her! What a terrifying thing this is! St Paul says the same of the pagan Roman Empire of his day (Romans 1:24; cf. Romans chapters 1, 2 and 3). God had warned in Genesis 6:3 that He would not allow His spirit to be *for ever* disgraced in man. The time comes when He withdraws, leaving the sinner in darkness (Hosea 5:15–6:1, Matthew 22:14) which is the result of his own actions. This plague would never have occurred if the king and Egypt had repented. To repent would be to choose the light and to choose the Lord, and to come under His rule in the Kingdom of Light or Kingdom of God.

Egypt was also being told that the sun-god she worshipped – Ra – was powerless before Him who is light, and the One who created light (Genesis 1:3). God's people in both Old and New Testaments are called 'children of light' (Ephesians 5:8), and Jesus showed Himself to be the light of the world (John 9:5); He said that anyone who followed Him would not walk in darkness - but in light (John 8:12). Today there are people all around us experiencing this same sign. If they have chosen to go the way of the world and sin they are in darkness, but if they have chosen the Lord and live in union with God's will they are in light. The light and darkness are all around us if only we have eyes to see (cf. 2 Corinthians 4:6). This message is also given clearly in Proverbs 4:18–19:

> The path of the virtuous is like the light of dawn,
>   its brightness growing to the fullness of day;
> the way of the wicked is as dark as night,
>   they cannot tell what it is they stumble over

The terrible darkness shows therefore that the Egyptians have no saviour, are excluded from membership of Israel, aliens, with no part in the Covenants with their promise, immersed in this world, without hope and without God (Ephesians 2:12).

Egypt was now ready to experience God's full judgement for sin. The final consequence of sin is death (cf. Genesis 2:17; Romans 5:12, 6:23). Death is the payment for sin. Jesus, our true saviour, paid the full wages for sin on the cross for us! He took the full guilt for all mankind onto His pure and sinless soul – 'became sin for us' (2 Corinthians 5:21). Part of this punishment for sin was that He was abandoned on the cross by His Father for three hours 'when there was darkness over all the land . . .' (Matthew 27:45). God had withdrawn from Him, and He cried out across the chasm that separated sinful man from the All-Holy God and was heard (cf. Psalm 22:24; Hebrews 5:7). 'My God,' He cried, 'why have you abandoned *me* – your Son?' (Matthew 27:47). And His voice was heard on our behalf (Matthew 27:46; Hebrews 5:7). But He had to take the final punishment for sin if He were to save us. He had to die.

Sin – darkness – death. This is the pattern we are dealing with in the plagues. It was only when Jesus willingly went into death and Hell for us that the full glory of God's light could break out on Easter Day to proclaim that 'God is Light' and that His reign had come to earth at long last.

You and I have the same choice before us as the Egyptians and the Israelites. We can choose to live in either darkness or light, and, whichever we choose, we must live out the consequences of our choice. Let us see the consequences for Egypt.

The final confrontation between Moses and Pharaoh (10:27–11:10)

Moses refused to leave Egypt without taking the Israelite livestock with his people (vv.25,26). Pharaoh would not give in; he ordered Moses to get out of his sight and never appear before him again or he would face death (vv.27,28). Pharaoh had made his choice at last. He had closed his heart to the Lord and His call, and God's messenger was put under threat of death.

Moses was undaunted, however! He responded to Pharaoh by declaring that he would not be back (v.29), but before he left the palace, God stopped him and sent him back to Pharaoh for the last time. There was to be one more plague, the death of the firstborn. This final dramatic scene between these two leaders amounted to a mutual sentence of death. But Moses' sentence came to pass. This was the final stroke of God that would bring Pharaoh and all Egypt to its knees, and begin the reign of the Kingdom of God on earth.

Moses went back to Pharaoh and delivered this final blow. Towards midnight tonight, he said, God will pass through Egypt as a destroyer; He will kill the firstborn of man and beast, from Pharaoh down to the least in the land. No one will escape (vv.4–7). Death would hang over Egypt like a dreadful executioner. But Israel would be saved. Oh, what a sting for Pharaoh! – to think that the royal heir to the throne would die and these miserable slaves – these nobodies – would be saved! (vv. 4–7; Romans 11:22). Pharaoh was now powerless before Moses – *this* plague would not be taken away. This was the end of the road and Pharaoh had lost. Every household in the land would have its dead that night, for sin in high places can have dire consequences. The pride and arrogance of this king had destroyed the people. The responsibility of those who govern, or indeed in any position of leadership, is very great. Moses said that after this event Pharaoh's courtiers would come to him, to *Moses*, bow low before him and beg him to leave! The courtiers would no longer follow Pharaoh; they would take the law into their own hands. Pharaoh was no longer ruler of Egypt, the Lord was – through His servant Moses – and the courtiers would acknowledge this (v.8).

And 'hot with anger' Moses left the presence of his defeated foe, knowing that he had won the conflict (v.8).

The tenth plague (12:29–34)
Just as Moses had foretold, death reigned over Egypt from midnight. Every household was struck, from the firstborn of Pharaoh, heir to the throne, to the firstborn of the prisoner in the dungeons, and the firstborn of all cattle. There was a great cry of distress and despair throughout all Egypt (vv.29–34). Pharaoh sent for Moses and Aaron while it was still night – obviously Moses was never too far away. They came and, wonder of wonders, heard Pharaoh give permission for *everything* that the Lord had requested! He said: 'You may go and worship the Lord – *and* take your flocks and herds with you!' (v.31). Now, not only could the people go but they could take all their possessions, they were not coming back.

Meanwhile the Egyptian people had taken the law into their own hands; they went to their Hebrew neighbours and urged them to leave Egypt quickly in case anything else happened (v.33). So the Exodus started that night, even before Pharaoh had sanctioned it.

Before leaving Egypt the Hebrews asked their Egyptian neighbours for silver ornaments, gold and clothing, and the Lord gave them such prestige in the eyes of the Egyptians, they were given anything they asked for (vv.35, 36). This is interesting. Obviously if the Hebrews were to survive as a people in the wilderness they needed these things for bartering. But God had promised them that they would not leave Egypt empty-handed and He always keeps His promises (3:21–22). Even Abraham knew this, four hundred years before the exodus: 'But I will pass judgement on the nation that enslaves them and after that they will leave, with many possessions' (Genesis 15:15). God has foreseen it all and made sure that His people would be provided for so that they could begin their new life in the wilderness. For four hundred long years this people had given free labour to Pharaoh and his people. I think that the Lord was saying that 'The labourer is worthy of his hire' – 'The labourer should be paid' (Luke 10:7; 1 Timothy 5:18). So these freed slaves were being paid in a lump sum for many long back-breaking years of hard labour that had made the Egyptians both rich and famous! The great stone cities of Pithom and Rameses spoke of this, and the great pyramids of Egypt still bear their silent witness before all the nations (1:11). The Lord is a just God, and impartial in His dealings with mankind.

It is interesting to note that God had given the Hebrews 'favour' or 'prestige' in the eyes of the Egyptian people. We see also in 11:3 that Moses had become a man of great importance in Egypt, held in the highest regard not only by Pharaoh's courtiers, but also by the whole people. The effect of God's dealings with them through Moses only gave the Egyptians an esteem, not only for Moses, but for his people. They were no longer despised as slaves, but respected as a people who had a very powerful leader in Moses, and a very powerful God in the Lord. The Egyptians, therefore, had come to acknowledge the Lord as the Living God and to fear His judgements. They began to respect His people as they witnessed how wonderfully He could protect them. So as they parted company for ever, the Egyptians showered gifts on their one-time slaves.

Why did God choose to punish the firstborn of all Egypt? Why not the guilty parents or the youngest in the family? Was there some special significance in the firstborn?

The firstborn of a family was considered in those days to be the representative of the family. He enjoyed certain privileges by the very fact that he was the first fruits of the marriage, and the child of his father's youth and vigour. He took precedence over his brothers (Genesis 43:33), and on his father's death received a double share of the inheritance (Deuteronomy 21:17) while automatically assuming head-ship in the family; his rights were protected by law against favouritism on the part of his father (Deuteronomy 11:15–17).

The firstborn, like the first fruits of the harvest, belonged to God (Exodus 13:11–15), so the greatest punishment God could give to a family was to strike down its firstborn – and this happened to every family in Egypt. Psalm 78 is a commentary on the exodus. It says that in killing the firstborn God destroyed 'the first fruits of their virility in the tents of Ham' (Psalm 78:51). In this plague God struck at the very heart of the nation.

It was a representative action. All the people were guilty but God had promised not to repeat the flood, when everyone perished (Genesis 8:21). Here the Egyptians as a people could survive, but the representative of the family had to die in their place.

At first glance this may seem very unjust until we study how the Passover took place. Briefly let me say here that the Israelites survived that night of disaster because a pure lamb was sacrificed instead of the firstborn. We, too, can survive the ultimate fate of our own sins because Jesus, 'the firstborn of all creation' (Colossians 1:15), 'the eldest of many brothers' (Romans 8:30), died for us on Calvary, having taken the full guilt of our sins upon Himself and paying the full price to set us free. Is this fair? Is it just, according to our standards? I think not! Why should Jesus die for sins He never committed? Why should I not have to pay the full price for my own sins? The answer lies in the Passover and in the privilege of life under God's Covenant. When we understand this a little more we should reverence the Lord, our dear Father, with gratitude and humility and enlist ourselves among His devoted servants.

5. The Passover: The Sacrifice that Sets Us Free

Chapter twelve of Exodus interrupts the flow of the narrative. The tenth plague was announced in chapter eleven, but is not carried out until chapter 12:29–34, and the intervening text gives us the instructions for the celebration of Passover, and the Feast of Unleavened Bread. The author (or authors) is telling us that the liberation of Israel from Egypt was the direct result of two separate major happenings on the same night, namely the killing of the firstborn of all Egypt by God, and the killing of the Passover Lamb by Israel. Israel had to prepare and celebrate Passover before the destroyer hit Egypt, or otherwise all the firstborn among the Hebrews would have died also!

The sentence of death given by the Lord through Moses was for everyone in Egypt: '*All* the firstborn in the land of Egypt shall die' (11:4). The Hebrews would escape because God would 'discriminate' between Egypt and Israel (11:7). This discrimination meant that all those who enter into covenant relationship with God through the Passover sacrifice will be saved, and those who do not will have to face God's judgement for sin, for 'the wages of sin is death' (Romans 8:22–23). This 'discrimination' put redemption between Egypt and Israel. Only those protected by the blood of the Lamb would be saved (12:23). In this way both God's justice and His mercy would be made manifest at the same time (cf. Romans 11:22) for everyone in Egypt – and that included the Hebrews, who were sinners. God is impartial in His dealings with us. God did not ignore or overlook the sins of Israel and choose to punish the Egyptians just to teach *us* a lesson! No! God never ignores sins. It was the blood of the Covenant entered into through the celebration of Passover that made the difference – for them and for us – God did not change! Jesus made the New Covenant in His own blood for us in His sacrificial death on the cross (cf. 2 Peter 2:3–10; Ephesians 2:3).

The Israelites were no better than the Egyptians in any moral sense. They were involved with the idolatrous worship of this pagan land, and before Moses' intervention on their behalf many of them had forgotten the Lord. Joshua was still trying to get them to give up idol worship even after their entrance into the Promised Land (cf. Joshua 24:14; Ezekiel 20:7–9).

We have already seen (in chapter 1) that their physical slavery manifested a deeper, more terrible bondage, namely the slavery of the heart to sin and evil. It was only as they slowly aligned themselves with the Lord and accepted the saviour He appointed for them that they began to experience His protection. (They had suffered the first three plagues along with the rest of Egypt.) It had nothing to do with any holiness or goodness on their part – no! they did not deserve His help. It was pure mercy on the part of God – love given to the undeserving.

St Paul tells us that it is exactly the same with us: 'all have sinned and have fallen short of the glory of God' (Romans 3:22–23). All of us deserve God's judgement for our sins, but when we enter into the covenant relationship with God through baptism and accept Jesus as our saviour and Lord, we begin to experience God's mercy and compassion to forgiven sinners. This goodness of God, our Father, towards us has nothing to do with any holiness or goodness in us. It was by sheer mercy that He saved us (cf. Titus 3:4–5; Ephesians 2:3–4).

Both for the Israelites and for us redemption centred around the death of a lamb. The fact that God accepted the death of the innocent lamb in place of His guilty people shows that He did not ignore their sinfulness. In fact, in order to appreciate the full glory of our redemption we need, first, to see clearly the moral depravity of the human race. If we refuse to acknowledge this depravity – if we try to minimize it by calling it something else – we will never really appreciate the magnificence of God's mercy to us in redemption, and thus we may never know the full joy and humble gratitude of the forgiven sinner. This is a tragedy, for we miss one of life's greatest blessings (cf. Romans 5:20; Luke 7:36–50).

The Passover Lamb (12:1–14, 21–28, 43–57)
It is obvious from the text that Israel had been prepared for this fateful night, when Egypt was to mourn her dead and Israel to rejoice in her salvation. They already knew that they were to celebrate a Passover in honour of the Lord (v.11). The word 'Passover' in our Bible comes from *pesah* in Hebrew or *pascha* in Greek (from which we got the expression 'Paschal Season' to denote Eastertide). The word means that God 'skipped over' the houses of the Israelites on the night of the tenth plague in much the same way that one would skip or pass over the names on a list. All the firstborn in Egypt were on the Lord's death list that night, but He skipped over the Hebrew names so that only the Egyptian firstborn actually died, and the Hebrews were ready for this.

They had been instructed previously to choose a lamb on the tenth day of the month Abib (later called Nisan), the month of the young ears of corn – March to April in our calendars – hence Eastertime. They were to hold it until the fourteenth day when it would be killed as the Passover Lamb. The lamb was to be sacrificed on behalf of a family and eaten immediately, so care had to be taken in choosing the size of the lamb (12:1–4).

The animal had to be without blemish, one year old – either a lamb or a kid. The assembled community were to slaughter the lambs at dusk and before sundown. Some of the blood was to be sprinkled on the two doorposts and the lintel of the houses. The flesh was to be roasted over the fire and then eaten with unleavened bread and bitter herbs.

Nothing was to be left to the following day. If they could not consume it all they were to burn it. They were to eat the Passover dressed in readiness to begin their journey into freedom, and the whole ceremony was to be carried out in haste (vv.6–11).

So, by midnight, when the destroyer came to Egypt, Israel was ready. Having sacrificed the Passover Lamb and fulfilled all of God's instructions, she was now protected from the tenth plague. As the Lord passed through Egypt that night and saw the blood of the lamb on the Israelite houses He passed over them (vv.12,13). God, therefore, accepted the sacrifice of the lamb and it was the blood of the lamb that made the difference between Israel and Egypt. Israel had been redeemed by the sacrifice of the passover lamb and was therefore 'covered' or protected by its blood. Egypt, on the other hand, had no protective covering to shield her from God's just punishment for sin. She was, simply, outside redemption!

To the modern person, especially in the West, animal sacrifice (which is still carried out in some parts of the world today) may seem to be a meaningless gesture, at most representing how *we* feel towards God. We wonder how the sovereign Lord of the universe, who has the heavens for His throne and the earth for His footstool (Isaiah 66:1), could value this type of ritual.

First we must see that God speaks to us in language and symbols and actions that mean something to *us*, otherwise communication would be impossible. We would not hear or understand Him. A mother, for example, communicates with her baby with gestures, signs and words that the infant understands; she will use different forms of communication with an adult. In both cases the persons involved must understand the language.

The language of the Passover is sacrifice, and at this stage of history, three thousand years ago, the normal expression of worship practised by all ancient peoples was animal sacrifice. Many of them offered human sacrifice too (cf.

Leviticus 18:21; Jeremiah 7:31, 19:5, 6, 32:35; Ezekiel 16:22; 2 Kings 16:3, 21:6, 23:10).

The people felt a deep-seated need to atone, or make up, to their gods for their sins, so we find that all pagan peoples worshipped in this way. The idea was to offer a pure victim to make atonement for the impurity of sin. The essential elements in sacrifice are as follows: first the people offer themselves to the god, then they acknowledge his sovereignty over them. There was always the element of the expiation of sins and offences committed against the god involved. By eating the flesh of the sacrificial animal they again entered into communion with their god, now that the relationship between him and his people had been restored through the sacrifice. A very important element was that life was transmitted to the deity by the death of the victim, and this life was then conferred upon the worshippers.

There was also the universal acceptance of the fact that blood represented life (since the loss of blood led to loss of life), so the blood of the animal was always given to the god as his portion of the sacrifice. The message of this gesture was 'we offer *our* lives to you and we acknowledge you as the Lord of life'. The blood was sprinkled on the altar or poured out at its base; alternatively it was smeared on the horns of the altar. The altar symbolized the worshipped deity.

This ritual of the blood is the precise symbolic act of oblation by which the life of the animal was transmitted to the deity. The mere killing of the animal would not suffice. This was followed by the eating of the flesh of the sacrificed animal to indicate entry into communion with the deity. The communion meal was the supreme symbol of fellowship with the deity and so it was a vital element in the ritual.[1] This was just one type of sacrifice. The Israelites had a whole range of sacrificial offerings as part of their worship, but we will only look at the meaning of the

[1] *McKenzie Dictionary Bible*, pp. 754f.

Passover sacrifice here. Let us look at each detail now and see what was communicated to God and to the people through it.

First, the lamb had to be killed (12:6) – the death of the innocent victim took place instead of the death of the guilty people. Second, its blood was not just to be shed, but was to be applied to the houses of any persons seeking protection from the destroying angel (12:13). Once the sacrifice took place and the blood was applied, what God would look for when He passed through Egypt was not any holiness on the part of His people but the covering of the blood of the lamb on their houses. The blood was therefore a very powerful signal between God and the people. The blood was to be applied using a spray of hyssop (12:22). The hyssop was an aromatic plant used only for the rites of purification of sinners (Numbers 19:6; Psalm 51:7; Hebrews 9:19; Leviticus 14:1–32). The fact that they used hyssop here in Passover is a statement to God that as sinners the Israelites sought purification as well as His protection. They would leave Egypt as a people cleansed of their sin and so become the Lord's army, the people of God.

Outside the realm of faith this makes no sense. What we see here is that the Hebrews at long last put their faith in the Lord. Their whole action on Passover night is an action of faith – killing the lamb and *expecting* God to protect them through its blood, entering into communion with God through eating the flesh, being dressed *ready* for all that faith told them God would do . . . as an act of faith it is a superb gesture, outside faith it is ludicrous (Hebrews 11:28). The people were still in Egypt, still under a stubborn king, but they are acting like a liberated people about to go on a journey. Not only did they put their faith in God – but also in the saviour He gave them, namely Moses (1 Corinthians 5:7). That night when they stepped out in faith they were saved! 'Your faith has saved you, go in peace' (Luke 7:50); 'If you had faith the size of a mustard seed you could speak to this mountain and cast it into the sea' (Matthew 17:20). That night their faith brought down the mountains of opposition, and they were freed to go out with God on their spiritual journey. What gave the Hebrews security in their homes that night was the blood of the lamb, but what gave them peace of mind and heart was the fact that they could trust God to keep His promises.

The Passover and Jesus: the Paschal Mystery

'Christ, our Passover, has been sacrificed; let us celebrate the feast, then, by getting rid of all the old yeast of evil and wickedness, having only the unleavened bread of sincerity and truth' (1 Corinthians 5:7–8).

Everything in chapter 12 of Exodus is a type of the Paschal Mystery. The Passover honoured the Lord: the death of Jesus, the True Lamb, gave great glory to God (John 12:28). Back in Genesis 22:8 we read that 'God would provide *Himself* a lamb'. This promise was made through Abraham after he made his supreme act of faith and trust in God in his attempted sacrifice of Isaac. That Lamb which God provided for Himself was Jesus; the sacrifice of Jesus would be the only sacrifice He would accept, replacing all other sacrifices (cf. Hebrews 9:11–14, 22–28). Jesus is the only pure victim accepted by God in place of all guilty people (Romans 8:32), and He neither needs nor accepts another.

The sacrifice of Jesus was a propitiation for sin rendered unto God – He paid the penalty for all of us, 'giving himself up in our place as a fragrant offering and a sacrifice to God' (Ephesians 5:2; Hebrews 9:26, 10:12; Romans 3:25–26). Therefore Jesus is our atonement, our lamb offered to God on our behalf, through whom we say to God 'we offer our lives to you and acknowledge You to be the Lord of Life' (John 1:29).

A sacrifice is also an offering of praise and thanksgiving to God (Jonah 2:10; Psalm 27:6; Hebrews 13:15). This is expressed at the Paschal Mass in this prayer:

Father, all powerful and ever-living God,
we do well always and everywhere to give you thanks
through Jesus Christ our Lord.
We praise you with greater joy than ever in this Easter
    season,
when Christ became our Paschal sacrifice.

He is still our priest,
our advocate who always pleads our cause.
Christ is the victim who dies no more,
the Lamb, once slain, who lives for ever.
(Easter Preface III, *Roman Missal*; see also IV, V, I)

The Church expresses praise and thanksgiving to God in and through Jesus in the re-enactment of His death sacramentally on the altar. Just as with the Passover Lamb, it is not enough that Jesus has died for us; we must enter into His sacrifice by appropriating its grace into our daily lives. The precious blood of the Lamb must be consciously applied to our lives, and we must live under its protective covering. This means that we can live permanently in His forgiveness, with His cleansing and healing power readily available to be used in all the events that make up our daily lives. Christians need to come to terms in a very practical way with the marvellous power given to them in the precious blood of the Lamb (1 Peter 1:18–19; 1 John 1:7).

It was a special lamb chosen from the flock four days ahead of time that was sacrificed. Jesus fulfilled this absolutely; He was chosen by God from among His own people and pointed out by John the Baptist as the lamb of God 3–4 years before His death (John 1:29; Exodus 12:3; Galatians 4:4).

It was to be a lamb without blemish (Exodus 12:5; Leviticus 22:21), as only a perfect sacrifice would be acceptable to God. Jesus was the sinless victim offered on our behalf (2 Corinthians 5:21; Hebrews 4:15–16).

The lamb had to be a male in its first year – this means a lamb in the fullness of its strength. Jesus died in the fullness of His manhood, possibly at forty years of age.[1] He was cut off 'in the midst of his days' (Psalm 102:24–25; NAB). The lamb was to be slaughtered by the whole assembly of Israel (12:6), and this is what we read in Mark 15:6–15. It was not just the Jewish leaders who put Jesus to death, it was the whole people, represented by the crowd before Pilate. It was because Pilate 'was anxious to placate the crowd' that he released Barabbas to them.

This incident of Barabbas and Jesus illustrates very well the principle of the innocent lamb dying for the guilty people (Matthew 27:17). A note on page 61 of the *Jerusalem Bible* New Testament tells us that the man's name was Jesus Barabbas. If this is so, then before the Jewish people that day stood a notorious sinner called Jesus Barabbas and also the all-holy Son of God, Jesus BAR ABBA, Jesus son of the Father. Pilate asked them to choose and the people chose that the innocent one should die and the guilty one go free. They unwittingly chose correctly, not knowing that Jesus was the Lamb of God who was to give His life for the salvation of all sinners, represented here by Barabbas (John 11:49–52). We do not realize the wonder of what happened here until – in prayer – we identify with the sinner and say 'I am that Barabbas, and Jesus died for me! He gave His life to save me' (2 Corinthians 5:14, 15; 1 Thessalonians 5:10; Galatians 2:20). Then we taste the joy and gratitude and praise of the forgiven sinner, loved with so great a love by God.

The lamb was to be slaughtered 'between the two evenings', that is, in the evening before sunset. At the time of the Exodus and long afterwards the lamb was killed at twilight, but by the time of Christ, because of the very large numbers of pilgrims who came to Jerusalem from all over the world, the ceremony had to be extended to allow for

---

[1] Christ was born circa 5–6 years BC. He was born before the death of Herod the Great in 4 BC, and spent several years in exile in Egypt, before Herod's death.

all the lambs to be slaughtered before sunset. John 19:14 tells us that the crucifixion of Jesus began at noon on the day of Preparation for Passover. Matthew 27:45 says that He died at the ninth hour, that is, 3.00 p.m. This was the day and the time at which the Passover lambs were slain in the Temple. Matthew further tells us that with the death of Jesus, the veil in the Temple which cut off the Holy of Holies was mysteriously torn from top to bottom, demonstrating the end of the Old Covenant and its Passover celebrations and the beginning of the New Covenant with the death of Jesus, the Lamb of God (Matthew 27:51). In killing the lamb they were not to break *any* of its bones. It was to remain intact (12:46) as a perfect victim, unlike other sacrifices (cf. Leviticus 1:6). John 19:36 points out its exact fulfilment in Jesus.

The flesh of the lamb was to be eaten by the community present for the Passover (12:8). They had to enter into communion with the lamb by appropriating it. Jesus, our Paschal Lamb, told us to eat His flesh and drink His blood or we would have no life in us (John 6:53). He communicates eternal life to us by our participation in Holy Communion (John 6:54). This eternal life is indestructible – death cannot destroy it (John 6:54). It is necessary for us therefore to participate fully in the celebration of the Eucharist. It has nothing to do with how we feel about it; the Eucharist is the food that nourishes us unto eternal life, in the same way as natural food nourishes the body regardless of how you *feel* about it. St Paul tells us to recollect ourselves before Holy Communion because our action in receiving it is a public proclamation of the death of Jesus until He comes in glory. He goes on to say that the sickness and death among the Corinthians was due to their wrong attitude towards the body and blood of Jesus in the Eucharist! (1 Corinthians 11:26–34). One of the signs of a healthy Christian community is its feeding at the Lord's table. But our participation must never descend to mere routine: if we consciously appropriate the grace offered to us we will grow spiritually. The communion was to go *with* the sacrifice on which it was founded. Communion is based on redemption which is already accomplished (cf. Luke 15:30).

The lamb was to be eaten with unleavened bread and bitter herbs. The bitter herbs normally signify suffering and, therefore, would be a reminder to the people that the Lord had saved them from the bitter bondage in Egypt. They would also remind them of the bitter suffering the Lamb had to endure to save them: the lamb could not be eaten raw or boiled: it had to be roasted over the fire. Therefore in order to save them the lamb had to undergo death and fire! Fire is used frequently in scripture to denote Hell and judgement, so the lamb had to undergo death and Hell to save the Israelites. Jesus had to suffer God's judgement for sin on the cross; the Creed tells us that He descended into Hell also. On the cross Jesus was not only the pure Lamb enduring death and Hell to save us; He was also the burning bush, enduring the fire of God's judgement for sin and He survived it in His Resurrection (cf. Galatians 3:13; 2 Corinthians 5:21; Jeremiah 11:19). The Church's 'bitter herbs' is her constant contemplation of the Passion of Jesus, keeping before her wondering eyes the terrible price paid by the Lamb of God in order to save us. Whenever we abandon the sight of His bitter pain we lose the joy of the celebration of the Eucharist and the wonder of the meaning of redemption.

The unleavened bread was the other accompaniment to go with the lamb and the bitter herbs. Leaven normally signifies something evil (1 Corinthians 5:6–8). In order to partake fully in the sacrifice of Jesus we must get rid of sin – especially deliberate, known sin – from our lives (Philippians 3:10; 1 John 1:7–10). The host that is used at Mass is made from unleavened bread, so when we walk up before the community to partake of Holy Communion it is not only a public declaration of the death of the Lord until He comes, but it is also a public declaration of our intent to break with sin and to live a life of holiness.

The Feast of Unleavened Bread went on for seven days, showing that God called His people to practical holiness in their daily lives. It was because they had now entered upon salvation or redemption that they must put away 'the old man' (Colossians 3:9), the old sinful ways.

As they ate the Passover they were to be dressed, with a girdle around their waist to tie up their long robes so that they could march easily. They were to have sandals on their feet ready for the journey, and a staff in their hands to help them walk (Exodus 12:11). The celebration of Passover signified the end of their slavery in Egypt and the beginning of their journey to the Promised Land. Our participation in the Eucharist also finishes with a commission to go out and *live* the wonder that we have celebrated. St Paul tells us in Ephesians 6:14–20 that the girdle around our waist enabling us to walk forth on our journey is *truth*. We go forth proclaiming the truth of who we are (sinners) and who He is (our saviour); we have integrity for our breastplate, protecting the heart and its loves, to keep it from going astray. The sandals on our feet are the willingness to spread the Gospel of peace to other sinners who need to enter into this Covenant relationship with God. The shield of faith is protection for the whole body, enabling it to stand and overcome temptation. The whole spiritual journey is a journey made in faith, and it is faith alone that overcomes the world in us and for us (2 Corinthians 5:7; 1 John 5:4). The helmet protecting our head and its faculties of intellect and will and memory is the gift of salvation; this will enable us always to walk in newness of life and prevent us from just intellectualizing our faith as distinct from actualizing or walking in it. The Word of God is our sword of protection, whether we are dealing with our own doubts or temptations or with the unbelief of the world (cf. Matthew 4). Finally we protect our spirit (soul, inward self) by continuous prayer (Ephesians 6:18), praying 'in the spirit on every possible occasion' and therefore praying in union with the will of God, and in the power of the Holy Spirit. This prayer is very effective for unleashing the power of God in our own lives as well as in the lives of others.

So we go forth from our celebration of Eucharist as the Israelites went forth from Passover, with our loins girt and staff in hand, walking in the power of God and under the protection of the precious blood of the Lamb, leaning on God in faith and trust to continue our journey, knowing that His grace is sufficient for us and that His power works best in and through our weakness (2 Corinthians 12:9). We carry the pilgrim staff in our hands; it reminds us that we do not have here a lasting city, that our homeland is in Heaven (cf. Philippians 3:20); Hebrews 11:13–16; Colossians 3:1–3; Hebrews 13:14). The staff also reminds us to go forward, leaning not upon ourselves or our own strength, but upon God.

They also ate the Passover in haste (12:11), for the Lord was coming to deliver them and they had to be ready. We, too, celebrate the eucharist as we 'wait in joyful hope for the coming of our Saviour, Jesus Christ'.[1]

'No foreigner shall eat it' (12:45–51)
There were clear instructions that no stranger or hired servant could participate in the Passover. The reason for this was that these would be outside the Covenant and could be worshippers of false gods. To enter into the Covenant all the males in the family had to be circumcised, then they were considered to be 'native born' and could participate in the Passover. (v.48). It is clear that the Passover was only for those who had entered into the Covenant relationship with God. It was the family of God's people celebrating their redemption and appropriating its grace and privilege into their lives.

St Paul reminds us in Ephesians 2:11–22 that the

---

[1] cf. Rite of Communion prayer after 'Our Father' in daily liturgy, *Roman Missal*.

Gentiles were all strangers and foreigners at one time, excluded from membership of Israel, aliens, with no part in the Covenant and its promise, immersed in the world without hope and without God. Having entered into the New Covenant of Jesus Christ through baptism, we can come to the Lord's table and participate in the New Passover in its re-enactment on our altars in the Eucharist. We are now 'part of God's household' (Exodus 2:19) and as such can participate in the family meal, celebrating our redemption in and through Christ and applying its grace to our lives.

For us, also, the stranger – the person who had not entered the New Covenant through baptism – is not allowed to come to our table and participate in the family meal of the Eucharist. He or she must first enter into the Covenant and be born again of water and the spirit (John 3:5) in order to be considered 'native born' in the family of God. We see here another aspect of Eucharist, namely that of the family of Jesus celebrating their new life around His table; our participation in it is our declaration to the world of who we are in Christ.

A day of remembrance (12:14)
The people were told that this feast was to be a day of remembrance for them for all generations. This, for them, meant that every year as they kept the feast it would not just be a 'memorial' but would be a re-enactment of the redemption in which the participants would re-live the events of the Exodus and keep its grace alive in their hearts. As a nation they were to go on into the future aware of the Covenant care and loving-kindness (*hesed*) of the Lord. Hence part of the celebration of Passover in the future would be the re-telling of the Exodus events to their children (12:27). All successive generations of Israelites felt themselves mystically united to the group who left

Egypt on the first Passover night.

The 'remembrance' was not just for the people – it was for God too! It would 'remind' Him of the Covenant He made with His people, and cause Him to continue to bless and protect them and guide them on into the unknown future. This is reflected in the prayers of the Passover meal.

The Eucharist is also a 'memorial' of the Passion and death of Jesus. The Last Supper was a Passover meal dominated by the impending horror of the Passion (Luke 22:7–13). 'Jesus said, "I have longed to eat this passover with you before I suffer; because, I tell you, I shall not eat it again until it is fulfilled in the kingdom of God"' (Luke 22:15, 16).[1]

The 'fulfilment' of the Passover entailed the sacrificial death of Jesus (Mark 10:45), so when He took the bread and blessed and broke it saying that it was his body, and likewise with the cup of wine that it was the New Covenant in his blood which would be poured out for us, He was clearly speaking the language of the sacrificed Passover lamb, claiming to be its fulfilment in His death (Luke 22:19, 20; 1 Corinthians 11:24, 25; Matthew 26:26–28; Mark 14:22–25). He was also showing Himself to be the Suffering Servant of God who would give Himself up in death to ransom the souls of many (Isaiah 52:13–53:12).

During the institution of the Eucharist at the Last Supper, Jesus commanded the Apostles to 'do this as a memorial of me' (Luke 22:19), and so ever after, when Christians met, the re-telling of what Jesus said and did on the night before he died was an essential part of their Eucharistic celebration (cf. 1 Corinthians 11:23–26 and the *Roman Missal*, the four Eucharistic prayers). With us, as with the Israelites, this 'memorial' is not just a re-telling of

---

[1]There is a discrepancy between this statement here and John's assertion that Jesus *died* on Passover Preparation Day. Whatever the problem, all the gospels are trying to tell us that Jesus is the new Passover Lamb.

the events of the greatest Passover night. It is a re-enactment of these events in which Christians are mystically united to Jesus and all that befell Him in His passion, death and resurrection, and they appropriate the graces of Jesus' victory on the cross to their daily lives. They also enter into Communion with Him by eating His flesh and drinking His blood, as He told us to do (John 6). In this way the Jewish Passover has been transferred into Christian Eucharist. From now on we no longer need to celebrate what happened in the Exodus, for we celebrate the true Passover that took place on Calvary and enjoy the fruits of salvation. The Eucharist perpetuates the sacrifice of the cross throughout the centuries until Jesus comes again. In it we have 'a sacrament of love, a sign of unity, a bond of charity and a paschal banquet in which Christ is consumed, the mind is filled with Grace and a pledge of future glory is given to us.'[1]

In this celebration we not only remember the Lord and re-live the Paschal Mystery but, like the participants in the Jewish Passover, we ask *Him* to remember *us*! We are His people, now living under the New Covenant, and we ask Him to 'remember' this and apply the fruits of it to us.[2] The pure victim that we offer to God in the Eucharist is the victorious lamb, now seated at the right hand of God and ever living to make intercession for us (cf. Revelation 5:6; Hebrews 7:25, 8:2, 9:24). The Father looks down upon His people covered and protected by the precious blood of the Lamb, and hears that victim's intercession on our behalf; we come away empowered to go forward on our spiritual journey with joy and hope and 'endued with power from on high' (Acts 1:8).

---

[1] Constitution on Sacred Liturgy No. 47, Vatican II.
[2] See the four Eucharistic Prayers in the *Roman Missal*.

A night of vigil (12:42)

Moses instructed the Israelites that the night when God kept vigil for His people in order to save them was to be kept as a vigil for all generations; on that first Passover night no one slept in Egypt: neither God nor the Israelites – nor the Egyptians! It was a night of vigil indeed, with so much happening for everyone involved. From henceforth, as they kept this vigil year after year down the generations, the people would not only look back to the marvellous deliverance of the Exodus but also look forward to the final deliverance of the people when Messiah came. It thus became both a memory and a hope, and the time of Passover became a time of heightened expectation of Messiah until the Israelites began to believe that He would finally make His appearance at Passover[1] (cf. Matthew 26:5; John 6:4,15).

This is also a part of the Eucharist: we look back to what Jesus accomplished for us on Calvary and we also look forward to His coming in glory and the final fulfilment of all things in Christ. His future glorious triumph has been part of it from the night of the Last Supper itself (Luke 22:15, 16; 1 Corinthians 11:26). We declare: 'Christ *has* died, Christ *is* risen, Christ *will* come again'. The early Christians cried 'Maranatha, come, Lord Jesus!' (1 Corinthians 16:22; Revelation 22:30). Just as the Passover for Israel belonged to the time between the Exodus and its fulfilment on Calvary, so the Eucharist extends from Calvary to the glorious final coming of Jesus.

One last point: In the solemn re-enactment of the mystery of the Passion, death and Resurrection of Jesus in Holy Week, various churches hold a solemn vigil on Holy Saturday night; this is the Passover vigil for Christians. It is a solemn night, a glorious night, and recounts for us all the wonders that God has done for us from the creation of

[1] cf. the Targun, a free Aramaic translation of the Bible.

the world, through the events of the first exodus from Egypt to the glorious redemption wrought for us by Jesus.

Exultant joy is expressed wonderfully in this Easter Proclamation, the Exultet; it is full of Passover imagery.

> For Christ has ransomed us with his blood,
>   and paid for us the price of Adam's sin
>   to our eternal Father!
>
> This is our passover feast,
>   when Christ, the true Lamb, is slain,
>   whose blood consecrates the homes of all believers.
>
> This is the night when first you saved our fathers:
>   you freed the people of Israel from their slavery
>   and led them dry-shod through the sea.
>
> This is the night when Christians everywhere,
>   washed clean of sin
>   and freed from all defilement,
>   are restored to grace and grow together in holiness.
>
> This is the night when Jesus Christ
>   broke the chains of death
>   and rose triumphant from the grave.
>
> What good would life have been to us,
>   had Christ not come as our Redeemer?
>
> Father, how wonderful your care for us!
>   How boundless your merciful love!
>   To ransom a slave
>   you gave away your Son.
>
> (*Roman Missal*, Easter Vigil)

This is a Christian song of triumph – a 'Red Sea Song', in which Christians give glory to God for the wonder of redemption wrought for us by Christ. As the Jewish community sing the song of Moses (Exodus 15) and celebrate the triumph of Passover and redemption at the Red Sea, longing for the coming and appearance of Messiah among them, the Christians at the same time celebrate the fulfilment of the Jewish rite, while longing for the final fulfilment of redemption at the *parousia* (Matthew 26:29; Luke 22:16). Together we sing the Song of Moses and the Lamb, even though it is in separate communities (cf. Revelation 15).

The consecration of the firstborn (13:1–2, 11–16)
One of the consequences of the Passover and the deliverance from Egypt was that God claimed all the firstborn sons of Israel as His own, so from that time the people had to 'sacrifice' their sons to God and 'redeem' or buy them back with a stipulated price. God is here laying claim to the firstborn, since He had saved them from death. St Paul told the Corinthian Christians that they were not their own property – they had been bought (redeemed) and paid for (1 Corinthians 6:19). The allusion is that Jesus our saviour redeemed us all from the slave markets of sin and now we belong to Him; He has the right of sovereign lordship over us which He exercises through merciful love and compassion. The redemption of the firstborn found its fulfilment when Mary and Joseph took God's own firstborn Son, Jesus, to offer Him to the Father; they 'redeemed' Him or bought Him back with the offering of the poor. Jesus was never priced very highly by man: as an infant He was bought for a pair of turtledoves and two young pigeons, and as an adult He was sold for the price of a slave (cf. Luke 2:22–25; Matthew 26:15, 16).

6. Deliverance at the Sea of Reeds

We now arrive at one of the most dramatic events recorded in the Bible, and one of the most important in the history of Israel – the night the Lord set His people free.

The Passover Lamb had been sacrificed, and all that God required of His people had been carried out. All that remained was for God to bring about the deliverance that the Passover signified, and this came speedily, for He always keeps His promises.

Pharaoh sent urgently for Moses during the night and ordered him to leave Egypt with all his people and all his possessions (Exodus 12:31). Meanwhile the Egyptian people had taken the law into their own hands and were urging the Hebrews to leave their country (12:34), so the Exodus of God's people from the land of bondage began on Passover night.

Preparations had to be made in haste, as there were flocks and herds in great droves to be taken (12:38) as well as an immense number of people of all ages. The haste was such that they took their kneading bowls with them under their cloaks with the dough in them – baked or unbaked! (12:34, 39). There were six hundred thousand men involved – not counting their families (12:37). The normal Hebrew census only counts men who are fit for fighting – never the old men or boys and never women or girls (cf. Numbers 14:30; Matthew 14:21). If this number represents a factual figure and you add a wife and two children to each one and allow for the old people, you will arrive at a figure close to two million! Add to this the fact that 'people of various sorts joined them in great numbers' (12:38) and you will understand why we are told that all the 'hosts'

(NAB, RSV) or 'array' (JB) of the Lord left Egypt that
night. The picture drawn for us here is one of triumphant
escape. Moses was leaving Egypt as the head of a great
army, with the men fully armed (13:18).

The mixture of 'people of various kinds' were obviously
Egyptians who had gone over to Moses, or slaves from
other nations who availed themselves of the general
walkout. But the fact that some may have been married to
Israelites (Cf. Leviticus 19:20, 24:10), and attached
themselves to Moses in this moment of triumph, is a strong
reminder of the parable of the dragnet and several other
parables of Jesus (related in Matthew 13) – the sower, the
wheat and the darnel. All of them show us that whenever
God intervenes in the history of man to do a new work
among us – for instance, at the Exodus, the birth of
Christianity and any renewal of the Church – the 'net' or
'seed' or message is thrown out to everyone, as the message
of Moses was preached to everyone in Egypt. The result is
'a haul of all kinds' (Matthew 13:47). At the beginning –
as with the wheat and the darnel – it is not possible to
distinguish between those who have sincerely responded to
God's call and those who have just followed the crowd in
order to be 'in on the action'. Later as events unfold you
can distinguish them 'by their fruits' (Matthew 7:16, 20),
namely the quality of their lives and commitment. The two
types are not separated until the judgement (cf. Matthew
13:41–43, 49–50). Numbers 11:4 tells us that this 'rabble'
who had joined 'the people' – thus distinguishing both
groups clearly – caused a lot of trouble for Israel. In fact
they were responsible for a major crisis among the people,
due to their greed (cf. Numbers 11:31–35).

The march to freedom (Exodus 13:17–22)
The Israelites set out from Rameses, the city of the sun,
which they had built as slaves, to begin a long journey to
an unknown future and a strange but promised land. This
speaks of God's call to the Church to come out from 'the

world' with all its vanity and all its toil 'under the sun' (Ecclesiastes 1:3), and to go on her spiritual journey through history to her strange but promised destiny in Heaven. For Israel this 'call' or vocation was given to her as a nation but for us it is given individually as well as collectively. Because of this the individual in Israel would rise or fall with the nation, but the individual Christian can achieve the Promised Land even if the group fails.

The Israelites' first stop was at Succoth, which means 'booths' or 'tents' – this highlighted their pilgrim state from now on. We too travel from our temporary homes here on earth to our permanent abode in heaven (cf. Hebrews 13:14; Philippians 3:20).

There were two routes open to them now. The shortest one – a matter of ten to twelve days' marching – went north along the Mediterranean coast through Gaza to the southeast of Palestine, called later in their history, 'the road to the land of the Philistines' (13:17). This was the usual road taken by both merchants and invaders, and it was well fortified by the Egyptian security forces. It is not difficult to see why Moses did not choose this way, for God had shown him that the prospect of fighting *all* the way to the Promised Land would be enough to make the people lose heart (13:17) and turn back. They were not ready for warfare yet; they were only beginners, spiritually. Forty years' training in the wilderness should prepare them to fight for possession of the Promised Land – but that time had not come yet! God takes us step by step, and mercifully does not show us all that lies ahead. If we follow His help and guidance at each stage we will be able to complete the journey without mishap. The tests given to those who are mature spiritually are not given to beginners; they would discourage them and cause them to turn back (cf. Psalm 103: 13, 14).

'God led the people by the roundabout way of the wilderness to the Sea of Reeds' (13:18). This route was the one chosen by God, and Moses, for the people. It led them *away* from Canaan, down south into a vast and terrible wilderness where they would sojourn for thirty-eight years before they attempted to go north into the Promised Land. They finally accomplished this two years later; thus the journey from Rameses to Jericho took forty years instead of two weeks!

The route went south-west of the Sinai Peninsula, parallel to the Red Sea (the Modern Gulf of Suez); it turned east at Mount Sinai and then north parallel to the Gulf of Aqaba. It ended at Elath. This is more or less the path of the Exodus, except that from Elath the people continued travelling northwards until they reached the Dead Sea, and entered Canaan at Jericho from the east side of the Jordan river.

It is important to see that God *led* them into the wilderness and through the wilderness to their destination. Jesus had the same experience before He set out on His ministry of salvation. In His whole life experience and ministry Jesus carved out a 'way' to the Father – a spiritual path which is safe for His disciples on their perilous pilgrim journey through life. He also gave us His 'truth' – the Word of God which was to be the lamp for our steps and a light for our path (Psalm 119:105), and He offered Himself as our sustenance, our 'Life' (John 14:6). Here in Exodus 13:21–22 we find that the Lord did just this for His Hebrew pilgrims. He went before them to show them the *way* (cf. Deuteronomy 1:33) and He guided them with His Word, given to Moses, and fed them on their journey (chapter 16). His special presence was shown to them in the *pillar* which manifested itself as a *Cloud* by day and a *fire* by night (13:21, 22). The continuous presence of God enabled them to persevere on their journey right to the very end; it was their greatest consolation on their way (cf. Exodus 40:36–38; Nehemiah 9:12; Numbers 14:14).

This personal presence of God and His special guidance was not given while the people were in Egypt. It began only as they set out on their pilgrim journey in faith and trust, and it stayed with them until the journey was completed. It points to the gift of the Holy Spirit to the Church, which was given after Calvary (Passover) as the young community set out on its pilgrim journey through history. The indwelling of the Holy Spirit is our 'Cloud' and is given to each person after baptism (our 'Red Sea') to accompany us on our personal journey as guide and teacher (cf. John 14:16–17, 26; 1 Corinthians 10:1–3). The gift of the Cloud was given to the Israelites without their asking for it, for they were not even aware of their need of its help. In the same way Jesus gave us the Advocate and Comforter without any request from us, for we too were ignorant of our need for this indwelling Spirit (John 14:16). The Cloud led the way through the trackless desert (13:21) so that the Israelites would never be lost, just as the Holy Spirit leads the children of God now (cf. Romans 8:14–16). The Cloud gave them light at night, just as the Holy Spirit is our light or enlightenment (cf. Nehemiah 9:12; John 16:13; Isaiah 11:2). God spoke to them from the Cloud (cf. Numbers 12:5; Psalm 99:7) and gave them His teaching and guidance just as He does today, through the Holy Spirit (cf. Acts, 15:28, 16:6; Revelation 2 and 3). At the Red Sea the Cloud gave a double manifestation. It shifted to the rear of the people instead of staying at their head, and separated them from the Egyptians. It showed itself as darkness to the Egyptians and as light to the Israelites (14:19–21), thus showing that only faith can perceive God's presence. Those trapped in the darkness of unbelief cannot discern or recognize this loving Presence, which is concealed from the proud and revealed to the humble ones (cf. Matthew 11:25; John 14:17).

The Cloud rested on the Tabernacle when the people pitched camp, and the glory of the Lord filled the Tabernacle (40:34–35). At His baptism the Holy Spirit rested on the head of Jesus, the One who came to tabernacle among us and He manifested His glory as the only Son of the Father (John 1:14). On Pentecost Day the Holy Spirit filled the young Church and henceforward showed His glory in and through them and their mission (Acts 2). No matter how sinful or unfaithful the people were, God never withdrew His presence from them. The gift rested on God's love and fidelity – not that of the people. We see this too in the history of the Church that the Holy Spirit has never been taken from us, no matter what we have done. Our great boast is the same as that of old Israel 'God is with us' (cf. Matthew 28:20).

The Israelites had to learn by experience how to respond to the Cloud until they reached humble submission to God's will in everything. This is expressed in Exodus 40:36–38, where we see that at each stage of the journey whenever the Cloud rose they would resume their march; if it did not rise they waited for God's timing. The Cloud became their signal to rest or to go on. Gradually we, too, learn to listen deeply to the Holy Spirit in our hearts and to respond with loving surrender. If we go ahead of what God is preparing for right now we find ourselves on our own, unsupported by grace, and disaster follows. If we wait patiently on the Lord and move when He tells us, then our progress can only be for the good, both to ourselves and others.

The path that God chose for His people led directly to the wilderness. It was His express will, therefore, that they should come to this 'Holy Spirit School' to learn all the spiritual lessons that were vital for their progress. The wilderness experience that had been so vital in the training of Moses was now to be extended to the whole nation. Like their leader they too were to receive God's Word in the solitude and silence of the desert; thus they became His first worshipping community (cf. Acts 7:36-39, 53) after their consecration to Him on the holy mountain. It was to be there, on Mount Sinai, that they would receive their rule of life from Him in ten words (the commandments), but first they must be tested and purified (cf. Deuteronomy 8: 2–6).

The crossing (Exodus 14)

This was the Lord's moment of glory, when He would play His trump card on Pharaoh and win for Himself everlasting glory. Israel treasures this moment as God's great sign of love to her in her moment of need (cf. Isaiah 51:15; Micah 7:15; Jeremiah 31:35; Joshua 24:6–7; Psalm 106:7–12; Wisdom 10:18–19). The event made a deep impression on the enemies of the Israelites as well as on other peoples who came to hear of it (cf. Joshua 2:10, 11), but like all the other great signs of God it can be grasped and understood only by faith. The people encamped between the wilderness and the Red Sea (14:1–2). The precise position of the crossing is unknown; it was somewhat north of the Suez Canal, in a marshy area. The people found themselves closed in by the wilderness on one side and the Red Sea on the other. News of their whereabouts was taken to Pharaoh; he was told that they were just wandering to and fro and that the wilderness had closed in on them (14:1–3).

Pharaoh regretted letting all his slaves go and decided to give chase taking with him six hundred of the best chariots, each manned by a picked team (14:5–8); this would have consisted of two warriors and a driver. He still did not realize that he was fighting with God, and also with 'the apple of His eye' (cf. Zechariah 2:8; Exodus 14:4). He seemed to think that his hour for vengeance on Moses had come as he approached Israel from the rear, trapping her people between his army and the sea.

When the Israelites saw the approaching army they became panic stricken – and turned to God in prayer, and to Moses in anger! (14:10–12). They had failed their very first test of faith. They should have put the lessons of the plagues into effect and trusted in God to protect them from Pharaoh, but no! panic had taken over. Trust in God is a hard lesson for us to learn and it only comes after many humiliating failures. In the spiritual life we seem to have very short memories of God's goodness to us in the past. As soon as a new trial comes upon us we behave as if God would let us down, as if He were *not* on our side! When we learn to trust in His goodness and mercy, disregarding our own merits, we go forward in peace.

As long as the Israelites looked back at Pharaoh and his army they were overcome with fear. When they turned to the Lord in prayer and trust, salvation came. St Peter learned this hard lesson on the night he walked on the water to Jesus (Matthew 14:22–23); see also Psalm 34:5–6, 17–20). Their cry to the Lord here (v.10) resembles that of the Apostles during the storm, 'Lord, save us, we perish!' (Matthew 8:26) and does not constitute a very good start to their forty years of life with God in a howling desert! They had forgotten that it was *God* who had led them to this place of testing and God would see them through, but their faith and trust had to grow and the testing furnished the circumstances in which this could happen (cf. Sirach 2; Philippians 4:19; 1 Corinthians 10:13).

In Pharaoh's pursuit of Israel we see an image of Satan, who is enraged at a soul delivered from his clutches and pursues it 'like a roaring lion' seeking to devour it (cf. 1 Peter 5:8–10). The soul, like Israel, now belongs to God and He will fight its battles. The Israelites are to discover that having God on their side means victory (Romans 8:31); but they have to learn to cling to God until the enemy is *completely* overcome. The soul often finds itself more tempted after its conversion to Christ than before, and becomes confused by this. As long as they were 'in the world' they were fine; they were in the enemy camp and did not experience Satan's hostility (John 15:18–27), nor did they have to face their own weakness as they do now in learning to trust God. They can also be filled with doubts and fears, so they conclude that they have got worse instead of better. This is a good sign even if a painful one, because it means that the fight is on for that person's soul just as it was for the Israelites. As with us, the Israelites had to realize that the Lord had not, in fact, set a trap for them, and that He would not let them down. They looked and felt helpless before their powerful enemies but it was the enemy – not the child of God – who was to face the terror of the Red Sea (cf. Revelation 19:20).

Moses stood in faith and trust before God and

challenged Israel to do the same (14:13-14). He spoke God's own word to them: 'Fear not!' This one message God has given to us over three hundred times in the Bible and has reiterated it all down the centuries of history (cf. Genesis 15:1; Joshua 8:1; Judges 16:23; 1 Chronicles 28:20; Isaiah 35:4; Daniel 10:12; Luke 1:13, 31, etc.). He asked them to stand still and watch how God would intervene to save them. This is a very difficult command to give to beginners in the spiritual life, when all our instincts tell us to 'do' something to save ourselves! Moses was demanding total surrender to God's will and providence for them; it looks like a suicidal action from the outside, but not for anyone who knows the tender-hearted love of God. Moses was certain that God would not let them down now after all He had done for them in the plagues and their aftermath.

But when we are in crisis the last thing we want to hear is 'Be still – and let God be God for *you*.' Our nature must be 'up and doing', in command of the situation, saving ourselves. The 'being still' sounds too passive. The Martha in us prefers to worry and fret about everything, forgetting the one thing that is necessary, which is this radical trust in God (Luke 10:41-42) and surrender to Him in all the events of our lives. Let Him work for us and in us and let us do only what He tells us (cf. John 14:31, 8:29). All this business of nature is only a manifestation of unbelief and a refusal to trust God; it leaves us with no permanent peace in our hearts. The permanent peace comes finally with total surrender to Him who loves and saves us. Faith and trust enable us to lift our hearts to God and to let His power come through. Just as there was nothing Israel could do to save herself from Pharaoh that day, so in time of difficulty and temptation there is nothing we can do except throw ourselves on the merciful love of God. Only God could control the wind and the waves of the Red Sea – as Jesus controlled the Sea of Galilee, and only He can calm the storms that assail us too. It was *only* by faith that Israel could pass through the Red Sea (cf. Hebrews 11:29). The moment the people opened up to real faith and trust, God opened up the Sea (Psalm 46:10).

God's response to Moses was to march on – into the sea! (v.15). Only faith could make sense of such a command, but the way forward in all our difficulties is not to change our circumstances but to work through the problem with the powerful grace of God to help us. There seems to be a contradiction between the command to 'be still' and to 'go forward', but they represent two stages in the working out of the problem. You have to 'be still' until you can deal with the problem in faith and trust; then the Lord opens to you the way forward that leads towards the solution.

Moses lifted his staff over the sea – the same staff used in all the signs in Egypt – and God responded as He did many times before. He drove back the waters of the sea by an east wind which blew all night (vv.16, 22). Meanwhile the Cloud changed its position to the rear of the Hebrews, thus preventing the Egyptians from making any headway (v.21). This gave enough time for the people to cross the sea as if it were dry land. Finally the Lord was shown as the same God who had divided the waters at the dawn of creation.

Water is a symbol of divine life and grace, so to say that the Israelites experienced 'walls of water to the right and to the left of them' is not only a poetic memory of the actual event, but points to all of us that the way forward is only possible when we are supported by God on all sides – 'Christ on my right hand and Christ on my left, Christ all around me . . .'[1] This way forward is perceived only with the eyes of faith.

The Egyptian army – but apparently not the Pharaoh himself – followed Israel into the Red Sea, and found to their dismay that the walls of water did not support *them*. As their chariot wheels became clogged in the mud they realized at last that the Lord really *was* fighting for Israel and against them (vv.24, 25). They retreated – but God

[1] cf. The Breastplate of St Patrick.

ordered Moses to stretch his hand over the sea again and the waters returned to the sea bed, capturing and killing all the Egyptians. The waters that saved Israel drowned the Egyptians, just as they had saved the good and drowned the wicked at the time of Noah (cf. Genesis 7:17–24).

This was the final break with Egypt for the Israelites; and it was the downfall of Pharaoh, who must have returned to Egypt a lonely and broken man.[1] St Paul says that this people was baptized unto Moses in the Red Sea (1 Corinthians 10:1–2), which points to baptism for us. When we walk into the waters of baptism it signifies our break with 'the world' and sin, the beginning of new life in Christ. Just as the Passover and the Red Sea are for ever linked in the liberation of Israel from bondage, so are Calvary and baptism for us. Our Passover Lamb (Jesus) has been sacrificed and we must appropriate the grace of redemption to ourselves by passing through the 'Red Sea' of baptism and actually stepping out to begin a spiritual life. As we meet with trials we can come through them victoriously by applying the lessons of the Red Sea – namely, to go forward protected by the blood of the Lamb and in obedience to the Word of God, in total trust.

The Song of Moses . . . and the Lamb
(Exodus 15 & Revelation 15)
This is the song that sprang from the hearts of a redeemed people in gratitude and praise of the saviour. Praise only comes naturally and easily to those who are conscious of their deliverance, and praise and joy are essential to worship. Those who are full of doubts and uncertainty about their relationship with God, who are not sure whether they are on the Heavenward road or not, cannot praise God: there is nothing to praise Him *for*. There are

[1]There is no historical evidence of any Pharaoh who died from drowning.

no songs of praise in Egypt – only sighs and groans – but now the Israelites rejoice and sing of their deliverance and their deliverer.

The key verse in this hymn of praise and thanksgiving is 'Who is like to you among the gods, O Lord? Who is like to you magnificent in holiness?' (v.11, NAB). The Israelites had learned the lessons of the plagues at last. The Lord is the God of Gods and this, the first 'Magnificat' recorded in the Bible, is totally God-centred, retelling the marvels of His mercy. For God had overcome their enemy in such a simple way that He showed them how easy it was for Him to save. Now they proclaim that the Lord is their salvation (v.2) and all His dealings with them were pure grace (v.13). The fame of the Passover/Red Sea events will spread worldwide and all their enemies will tremble (vv. 14-16; cf. Exodus 18:10–11; Joshua 2:9–10, 9:9; 1 Samuel 4:8). They now believed that God would keep the rest of His Promises to them (vv. 17–18). Now that the Lord had purchased them – another expression for 'redeemed', but this time meaning 'bought back' – they were His people and He was their King and Lord as well as Saviour (vv. 16–18). This declaration of praise was followed by the women – led by Miriam, Moses' elder sister – dancing with their tambourines to express the joyful worship of the people.

This song of triumph was sung to celebrate the beginnings of redemption. The Book of Revelation tells us that the redeemed in Heaven will sing the song of Moses *and* the Lamb to celebrate the completion of redemption as worked out in the history of man. Just as the Israelites praised God for overcoming the Egyptians, so the saints praise God for overcoming the true enemy, symbolized in the beast (Revelation 15:2–3). Jesus is called the King of Nations, just as the Lord was here called the King of Israel.

The song of victory closed the first half of the experience of Israel in redemption. It also marked the beginning of their new life in the Lord. When they had finished singing and dancing they had to turn around and face the vast and terrible wilderness that lay ahead of them, and to begin their life of faith and trust in God.

For many who have experienced renewal in the Church today, this 'Red Sea stage' can be a snare. The praise, singing and rejoicing heard everywhere in prayer groups celebrates all that Jesus our Saviour has accomplished for us in salvation. This is wonderful as far as it goes, but we must not stop there. Every stage is only a stage that we must pass through, but the Lord calls us ever onwards. We must not be afraid to face the pain of growth to spiritual maturity, nor flinch from the purification that is necessary to arrive at union with God. There was to be little evidence of singing and dancing as the Israelites traversed the trackless wasteland: they would muster all their energies just to keep trusting in a God of Love who allowed them to suffer so terribly, and as we already know, they failed every test of God in that school of the Holy Spirit! (cf. Psalm 95:8–11).

The Promised Land still lies in the future, so to remain at the Red Sea would frustrate the designs of God for them – and for us. When we come to personal conversion or renewal in our own lives, it is only the beginning; we must not hold on to any of our experiences of God, no matter how great. We can rejoice and give thanks; we then move on to the next stage of the journey where we will experience more of God. We must persevere until we have set foot in the Promised Land. Nothing must separate us from the Love of Christ – not even our greatest experience of Him! We move on single-mindedly towards our goal.

III. The Time of Growth

7. Training in the School of the Desert

First cycle of growth (Exodus 15:22–27)
Moses ordered Israel to break camp at the Red Sea and march into the wilderness of Shur, where the Israelites faced their first test. For three days they travelled without any water (v.22). Physically the temperature, combined with the exhaustion of travel in a dusty desert, made this a very severe test. Old and young suffered severe thirst, but they were after all in a wilderness. However, while thirst can be expected on a physical level, almost nobody thinks it should be so on a spiritual level.

The early stages of the relationship with God are characterized by powerful feelings. When you pray you may have a strong sense of peace and joy, of the presence of God. Such feelings are called 'consolations'. At this level we may not realize that we are carried along by those experiences rather than by a pure seeking after God Himself. For instance, to be freed from some serious problem in your life is a very *felt* thing. The experience of God's forgiveness or the forgiveness of another person is also a powerful emotional release, and healing, either emotional or physical, is a plainly visible sign.

The first lesson of the school of the desert takes away these consolations; you feel dry, arid and unable to pray as you used to. You get no satisfaction out of prayer or spiritual things any more. If you belong to a prayer group,

131

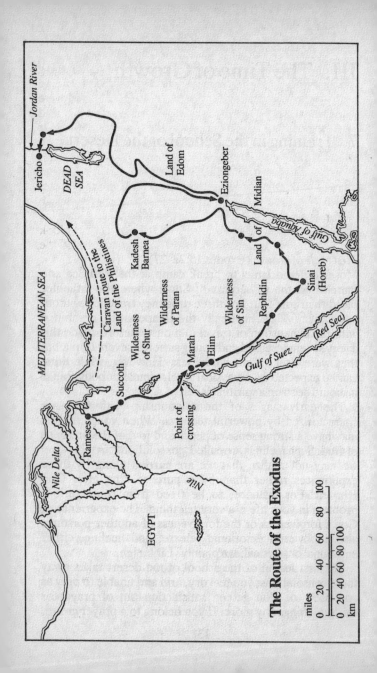

The Route of the Exodus

you may develop a distaste for loud praise and singing because you do not *feel* like singing. Instead you feel 'like a dry weary land without water' (Psalm 63:1). You are experiencing need and if you do not learn why this is so and what to do about it, you may sin as the Israelites did. Your need comes from a sense of God's absence, even though He is always with you (Matthew 28:20; Psalm 139:7–12). You have to learn to seek Him for Himself alone rather than to seek Him for His gifts (Hosea 6:1), but this comes slowly. We have to learn from experience to distinguish between the gift of the lover – in this case water – and the love of the giver. Like an infant we have to learn to look up from the mother's breast to see the person behind the gift.

This is the start of the 'school of the Holy Spirit' – the training period for all those who really *want* to reach the Promised Land, and the lessons begin immediately. The purpose of the lessons, or testings, is to show up what lies hidden in our hearts – often unknown to ourselves (cf. Deuteronomy 8:2–6) – and therefore to humble us, making us turn to God, dependent on His mercy instead of reliant on ourselves. They also show us that we do not deserve all that God does for us, that we do not merit it by any goodness on our part. Both redemption and sanctification are a work of His mercy alone, and the whole process glorifies His great goodness towards us – 'the goodness and kindness of God our Saviour' (Titus 3:4).

The problem for us is that these testings show up our weaknesses and sinfulness; and we do not like this. Self-knowledge is bitter medicine to us, so we complain and grumble and seek avenues of escape from God's purifying fire. But this same self-knowledge lessens our self-esteem and shows up our independence of God, which, we hope, will make us throw ourselves on God's mercy so that we know Him as the source of all our good. Experience shows us that the self gives way only very gradually before the onslaught of the divine fire; a great struggle ensues between the soul and God (cf. Romans 7:14–24). The soul wants God, but not on His terms; it keeps on trying to have things its own way, while God pursues it like a relentless lover. If we do not give up, He will show us the wisdom of His ways and will enable us to surrender to Him so that His grace can triumph in us (cf. Romans 15:5, 16:25).

It is the testing of the wilderness that shows up the true corruption of the heart, showing why the sign of the leprous hand was for those about to submit to the process of salvation. Israel had been saved from Pharaoh, but the wilderness will show her a more terrible enemy residing within. It is self! It comes as a shock that we have to be delivered from ourselves! The work of sanctification – or the final deliverance of the soul – is the liberation from the tyranny of self. As long as the self has not surrendered to God, the reign or kingdom of God has not been fully established, the victory is not fully experienced by us, and we are only half-redeemed.

The half-redeemed are in real misery, but can be seen all around us in the Christian world of today. They are people who have been saved by Christ on the cross, but have not entered personally into the mystery of Christ so that they can experience all the redemptive graces available to them. They do not enter into personal relationship with Jesus, nor surrender the inner fortress of the self so that union with God becomes a normal part of their lived experience. They are a poor advertisement for Christ, for they neither seem nor behave as if they are redeemed, and the song of praise is foreign to them. They do not know the meaning of the promise of John the Baptist: 'He will baptize you with the Holy Spirit and fire' (Matthew 3:11). For this purifying fire to work in us we must face into the wilderness and all that it holds for us. The transformation wrought in us by the desert is expressed wonderfully in the Song of Songs (8:5):

> Who is this coming up from the desert
> leaning on her Beloved?

Only the desert can teach us the true meaning of God-with-us. There we find that He does, indeed, supply all our needs as lavishly as only God can (Philippians 4:19). The wilderness not only teaches us about ourselves but also about Him whom our souls love. The growing relationship with Him teaches us all we can grasp about the I AM who is with us. We learn that He is Father, provider, healer, teacher, guide, protector, our shield, our light, our hope, our glory and our heaven, our destiny (cf. Ephesians 3:16–20). These are the revelations we receive in the school of the Holy Spirit where we are all taught by God (John 14:16; 1 John 2:27; John 6:45) through personal experience. Those others who have not passed through this school know these things as 'doctrines' or knowledge gleaned from books, but for the desert people it is their daily bread. They also can say 'God is our *Father* . . . He fed us with Manna – we drank water from the rock [we did not *read* about it] . . . the clothes on our back did not wear out all those forty years' (cf. Deuteronomy 1:31, 2:7, 8:4). To emerge victorious from this test is to become a radiant disciple who can give first-hand testimony about the Living God. You show by speech and behaviour that you belong to God's family and that you speak out of your sonship (Romans 8:14). This draws others to leave their campsite and enter the desert school so that they can join the royal line of all those who have known God and loved Him and served Him unto death – for it is impossible to come to know this great Father without loving Him, and equally impossible to know and love Him without feeling His longing for all His children to come and experience the fullness of redemption (cf. John 17:3, 18–23). It is our Joshua (Jesus) who takes us from the desert to the Promised Land. It is leaning on the arm of this bridegroom, as Christ called himself, that the Church will enter into glory, to the amazement of all her enemies.

The entrance to the desert for us begins when we take hold of our privilege in Christ and begin consciously to let the Lord work in us, when we stop demanding that the controls of our lives remain in our own hands and begin really to surrender to His will in real obedience of the heart . . . 'not my will but thine be done . . . be it done unto me according to your Word . . . let your Word come to life in me . . .' expresses the interior disposition. We begin to give real fidelity to daily prayer, listening to God's will to be shown to us. We open up our hearts to make a home for the Lord and His Word (John 14:26).

We can experience the wilderness in two ways: firstly, as it relates to the world. Secondly, as it relates to God.

As soon as we begin to grow spiritually we see the world for what it really is. Before, we found the world a lovely place to live in, but now we see through its glitter and glamour to the awful emptiness that is really there. We see the corruption all around us, even in good people, and we are nauseated by it. While we were mixed up in it we did not see it, but now we see the masks people hide behind and the sin that is everywhere; we begin to understand St John's words: 'You must not love this passing world or anything that is in the world. The love of the Father cannot be in any man who loves the world, because *nothing* the world has to offer – the sensual body, the lustful eye, pride in possessions – could ever come from the Father but only from the world; and the world, with all it craves for, is coming to an end; but anyone who does the will of God remains for ever' (1 John 2:15–17). Through the eyes of faith we begin to see the world as a desolate wilderness – a place that we must leave in order to seek God and God's Kingdom. And so we begin to feel unsettled; we join the royal line of 'strangers and nomads on earth' seeking for the eternal City (Hebrews 11:13–16). This search began with Abraham and each one who follows him must become a Pilgrim setting out for the heavenly homeland. More and more as we follow the Lord we find ourselves acting on different principles to those in the world; we can feel estranged from them. In the world you give as good as you get, but you learn in the school of the wilderness to respond to life's hurts with forgiveness. In the world it is acceptable to be a 'grabber' a 'go-getter'; it's acceptable to walk over others to get to the top of the social or financial ladder. But here we learn to give and be generous with others – it's a very different 'world' or 'kingdom' or way of life that the Lord teaches His children. The world is a hard, cold and uncaring place where injustice flourishes and the poor have no place. Those who come to the school of the wilderness learn compassion and love and are directed to wash the feet of their poor neighbour. Yes, the world and the wilderness are two very different places and those who enter deeper and deeper into the way of the Lord feel the hatred of the world directed at them just as their Master did (cf. John 15:18–21).

The extraordinary thing about the experience of the wilderness is that, while it detaches us from the allurements of the world and shows up its empty glitter, thus releasing us from its stranglehold . . . at the same time the wilderness makes us feel far from God! It shows up *our* sinfulness too and makes us feel distant from Him – whom we then begin to seek with all our heart! This feeling of distance from God is the source of all our discontent in the wilderness. We feel desolate – not only cut off from the world, but somehow abandoned by God because we do not have the very immediate experiences of Him which we felt in the early days. We think that all is lost, not realizing that the trials of the wilderness are preparing us for the much deeper graces and more wonderful manifestations of God. But this is poor consolation for those in the midst of the trial. They feel that *their* case is different and that they are not understood – that God has abandoned them! You see, there is *no water* and that is that! This is very unsettling and disturbing; for how could this lack of peace come from God? Well, it could! One of the false notions many people have is that our relationship with God should be peaceful and quiet all the time. If it were no growth would be taking place. If there is growth, there is movement. Growth from one stage to another demands an openness to be challenged and changed, and of course the adjustment stage is unsettled. The 'peace' we have must be real, not an absence of life and growth (cf. Hebrews 12:5–12).

The lack of water on the journey creates in us a thirst for God Himself; in the early days we would have been satisfied with His gifts and graces. Now the soul begins to thirst for *Him* and tastes the fact that nothing can satisfy the human heart but God alone: 'In God *alone* there is rest for my soul' (Psalm 61:1). Psalm 63 expresses the thirst that increases with time and experience of the Lord:

> God, you are *my* God, I am seeking *you*,
> my soul is thirsting for *you*,
> my flesh is longing for you,
> a land parched, weary and waterless;
> I long to gaze on you in the Sanctuary
> and to see your power and glory.
>
> (Psalm 63:1–2)

We come to learn slowly that God alone can slake that thirst, but this wisdom does not come overnight. In the exodus the Israelites are at the stage of the Samaritan woman Jesus spoke to and offered living water: '. . . but anyone who drinks the water that I shall give will never be thirsty again: the water that I shall give will turn into a spring inside him, welling up to eternal life' (John 4:14).

The dreadful drought of the soul can be healed only by God, who supplies all its needs. For the person who perseveres through this trial, trusting in God's goodness instead of murmuring and complaining, and who pierces the Heavens with his cry of thirst for God, will have his prayer answered abundantly, when the time is ripe. God will eventually make *him* into a source of life and grace for others – as He did for Moses. Moses could not have led a whole people through the vast wasteland if he had not himself trained in it beforehand and discovered that faith and trust and perseverance are the essential equipment for crossing the desert. Without faith and trust and a firm refusal to give up, we would fail and might even die in the wilderness, as many of the Israelites did. But this is not necessary: God did not call them to die in the wilderness, though they often accused Moses of leading them into the wilderness just for this (Exodus 16:3, 17:3; Numbers 20:2; Exodus 16:2; Numbers 11:4, 14:2).

Jesus also had to undergo the test of the wilderness. It seems to be a 'must' for the servant of God. But instead of forty years Jesus spent forty days in hunger and thirst and lonely seeking after God His father. When we study Him we see clearly how *we* are to survive this testing period. No complaint was found on His lips, for His heart was truly surrendered to the Father's will: '. . . the world must be brought to know that I love the Father and that I am doing exactly what the Father told me' (John 14:31). So with humility and trust He stood up to the tempter and defended Himself with the scriptures – putting God's word before Him as a defence (cf. James 4:7). 'Man does not live on bread alone, but on every word that comes from the mouth of God' (Matthew 4:4). He set aside His own hunger, denied Himself His right to eat . . . and later God made *Him* the Bread of Life, the source of nourishment for all His children. He set aside honour and glory and political stength, and God made Him King of Kings and Lord of Lords! (cf. Matthew 4:8–11; Revelation 19:16). We see illustrated in Him the principle that 'he who humbles himself will be exalted' (Luke 14:11).

St Luke tells us that Jesus came out of the experience of the wilderness triumphant, 'with the power of the Spirit in him' (Luke 4:14). In all the ways that the children of Israel had failed, Jesus had triumphed, showing us that complete surrender to God in faith, trust and humility is the way forward. Jesus carved out a path in the desert all the way home, back to the Father: 'I am the Way . . .' (John 14:6). He is our beacon light, and following Him we do not get lost (John 8:12). And He alone has the water of life for us.

The waters of bitterness (15:24–26)

The people suffered a severe drought for three days. They were desperate for water, but when they found water at Marah it was so bitter that they could not drink it. Their frustration knew no bounds, and they grumbled against Moses. Moses appealed to the Lord on their behalf and the Lord showed him a tree; Moses threw some of its wood into the water to sweeten it. We see God's providence at work here, providing for His people's need.

This trial came very soon on the journey, and we almost forget that it is only a few days since the people sang and danced to God at the Red Sea, for all the wonders He had done for them! That is all forgotten now in their first trials. They gave the impression in their song of triumph that their trust was real, but it was only real when they saw their enemies dead on the shore (cf. John 4:48) – when they saw results. Real trust shows itself before any results are seen: 'Blessed are those who have not seen and yet believe' (John 20:29). All the complaints and murmurings that *we* make against others and against the circumstances of our lives show up the same lack of trust in the Lord who guides us by a sure hand to our destiny beyond the wilderness. We need to have our spiritual eyes opened to see beyond the immediate, we need to keep our eyes on the Lord. The bitter experiences of our lives are meant to drive us into the arms of the Lord so that we discover in Him an unfailing supplier of our every need, and to detach us from seeking God for what He will give to us until we can seek Him for His own sake.

Commentators differ in their treatment of the way in which the water was sweetened by the tree. Some dismiss it as if it was not significant; but it does have deep significance. The 'wood of the tree' speaks of the Passion of Christ. Nothing can sweeten the blows of life for us unless we take shelter underneath the cross – the tree – of Christ. If we are to grow in the likeness of our crucified

Master then we must know that suffering is part of our privilege as Christians 'And if we are children we are heirs as well: heirs of God and co-heirs with Christ, sharing His sufferings so as to share His glory' (Romans 8:17). If we are to come through our trials successfully we must embrace our cross, which is ourself, with all its weakness, and embrace the circumstances of our lives and let God work with us (Ephesians 2:10). But if we grumble, complain and resist we frustrate God's designs for us and make ourselves and those we live with truly miserable. If we embrace the shame of being less than we would like to be in our own eyes and the eyes of others, and stand naked before God's truth, we find Him merciful and loving. He knows that we are dust . . . and never treats us as our sins and faults deserve (Psalm 103).

If we can meet the trials of every day with praise and thanksgiving in our hearts, and surrender to God's will and providence for us, we shall find victory through the cross, and great peace and joy. The early Christians knew this and could rejoice in their trials and suffering (cf. Acts: 4:31, 5:40–41, 7:55–60, 16:25–34).

The Will of God – our rule of life (15:25–26)
It was here in the midst of their first trials that God showed Israel that He was Lord over them, and that their lives must be governed by His will.[1] God was not calling them into a kingdom of chaos, where everyone would do his own thing. No! He was calling them into His kingdom where He would reveal to them His Law, by which they would abide. It would be in the keeping of His law that they would find life and healing and give an acceptable service to God. God was setting up the only theocracy that ever existed, and He had the governmental rule of Lordship which He exercised through His servant Moses. Therefore He said:

[1] His will is also called law, statutes, commands, ordinances, etc.

141

If you listen carefully to the voice of the Lord your God and do what is right in his eyes, if you pay attention to His commandments and keep His statutes, I shall inflict on you none of the evils that I inflicted on the Egyptians, for it is I, the Lord, who give you healing. (v.26)

So from the very beginning God required obedience to His will or His laws as the sign through which He would bless His people; and it is the same for us under the New Covenant. Jesus said, 'If you love me you will keep my commandments' (John 14:15). Obedience is the acceptable sign of love to God, but rebellion against God's will is what caused Israel's problems both in the wilderness and in the Promised Land. And it is no different for us because in God's will lies all our perfection. Our stubborn independence – 'wanting to do our own thing' – brings much trouble and unnecessary pain upon us. But it takes wisdom to recognize the rightness of God's ways and dealings with us. It is in the living out of God's will for us that we find true health and wholeness – for He becomes our life, our health, our living water, and our bread! He becomes all to us.

Rest at Elim (15:27)

Soon after this the people came to Elim, where there were twelve water springs and seventy palm trees. This is a very short statement of a wonderful event in their lives. It was their first relief from the rigours of the desert, and represents the rest periods of our spiritual journey. Water is a symbol of divine life given to us, and wells of water or springs of water represent the abundance of that life available to us. Jesus promised the woman of Samaria that He would put a spring of water inside her to bubble up to eternal life (John 4:14). The number twelve signifies the fullness of Israel – the twelve tribes – and the seventy signifies the full leadership of Israel – seventy elders – the same numbers that Jesus chose for His twelve apostles and seventy others (some say seventy-two) (Luke 10:1 and note b; JB).

The Lord leads His weary pilgrims to the waters of repose in order to revive them there (Psalm 23:3), so it is a time for refreshment and restoration and peace before taking up the ardours of the journey again. It is a brief taste of what things will be like, permanently, when the Israelites reach their goal. Then they will be described as trees planted by streams of living water, bearing plentiful fruit (Psalm 1:3; Revelation 22:2). But this is a far off ideal at this stage; the people have a lot of growing to do to reach it. We see here the Lord's goodness to us; He allows us a brief taste of what is to come in order to draw us further along the spiritual way.

8. Food for the Journey

The Lord led His people into a desolate region where survival is a major problem for all travellers, but for the huge multitude that left Egypt under the leadership of Moses it was an impossibility. If God would not provide food for them they would starve to death. The Book of Numbers, chapter 33, tells us of the various stages of the journey from Egypt to the Promised Land. The Book of Exodus does not record all these stages because they covered no significant event. Only those events that show a development in the relationship between the Israelites and God are recorded. After Elim they encamped by the Sea of Reeds before entering the wilderness of Sin (Numbers 33:11); soon the shortage of food became critical. The full impact of desert life had its effect only after the relief of Elim and the Sea of Reeds, and it was *more* difficult because of this.

This is so true of the spiritual life; we find discipline and privation more difficult after a period of rest. It is this very change from one state to the other that shows up the deeper layers of sinfulness that lie hidden within us, unknown even to ourselves until the right circumstances come along! This initiates the second cycle of growth (16:1–2).

The whole community complained against Moses and Aaron, saying that it would have been better to die at the Lord's hand in Egypt than to face the slow starvation of the wilderness. In their panic, imagination took over and they claimed that they had had pans of meat and bread to their heart's content in Egypt! Chapter 11 of the Book of Numbers shows them reminiscing about the fish, cucumbers, melons, leeks, onions and garlic (Numbers

144

11:5). To indulge the imagination like this is dangerous. At the very least it takes away our ability to face the reality of our situation, and leaves us in a negative mood, unable to cope. I doubt that the taskmasters of Egypt had fed their slaves so well!

How quickly Israel had forgotten the wonders of the Lord, both in Egypt and in the Red Sea. Could not He who opened the sea for them provide bread from Heaven? But in their panic they did not pray! They did not *ask* the Lord to provide their daily bread, as Jesus told us to do. We see here how important it is for us, in our moments of crisis, to reflect back on all that God has done for us and then trust Him to be God for us now, in the present. But no! Spiritually speaking we have very short memories. We think, 'He won't do this for us'. Panic comes easier than trust.

Moses turned to God for help. With his long experience of the wilderness he knew that God was the Israelites' only source of hope, so he calmly spoke to the God who not only saves His people but nourishes them for their new life. The Lord's reply was wonderful – 'I will rain down bread for you from heaven'! This meant that He intended to give them a plentiful supply of bread. But in the giving of the gift there would be a test of faith and trust so that the people could grow (vv.4–5). God attached a command to the giving of this bread from Heaven: each day they were to gather just enough *for that day only* – no provision for the morrow. (How difficult this would be in a wilderness!) There was to be but one exception. To respect the law of Sabbath rest God would give them a double portion on the Friday (vv.4–5).

Moses and Aaron gave God's reply to the people. They said that in the evening there would be a new manifestation of the Lord, and the following morning they would see His glory! In the evening they would have meat to eat and in the morning bread to their heart's content (vv.6–8). Moses added that their lack of trust in God was not a good sign at this stage; they were already showing signs of stubborn refusal to believe unless God continued to show them signs and wonders (John 4:48). They should be growing in understanding and trust instead of behaving like demanding children.

The Book of Numbers gives a very unflattering account of how the quails were provided by God. Numbers 11:4 tells us that the rabble who had joined Israel (cf. 12:38) and were overcome by greed were the cause of the trouble which eventually spread throughout the whole camp. It tells us that Moses found difficulty in believing that God could provide meat for such a crowd (Numbers 11:21–23), but that when the gift came it was given in great abundance. The Lord drove quails in from the sea until they lay on the desert floor two cubits thick on the ground![1] But those who indulged themselves with this meat fell victim to a plague. God's gift is never given for self-indulgence, so the blessing turned sour on them (Numbers 11:31–34).

Commentators say that the manna and the quails were a 'natural' event. Quails migrate across the desert from North Africa to southern Europe. Manna, they say, is a secretion from insects which live in the tamarisk tree. This may be so, but the sheer quantity of each substance provided for the people was not natural. The desert would have to become a fertile land to provide for such a multitude every day, and how would the insects know that they were to provide a double portion on Fridays and none on Saturdays? No! This is the hand of God providing a table in the wilderness for his starving people (cf. Psalm 23:5, 78:19–31). This was the banquet in the wilderness that they had challenged Him to provide!

---

[1] A cubit is taken as either eighteen or twenty-one inches. The quails were therefore three feet thick on the ground!

Manna from heaven

The people had been told that they would see the glory of God in the provision of manna (16:7), but what they actually found the following day was clearly a disappointment to them. Whatever their imaginations had conjured up, the reality was very different!

When the dew lifted from the desert the following morning they saw 'a thing, delicate, powdery, as fine as hoarfrost' on the ground, and they said to one another 'What is that?' 'That,' said Moses, 'is the bread the Lord gives you to eat!' (vv.14–15). They were puzzled and disappointed. How could this 'thing' be a manifestation of the Glory of God? They called it 'man hu' which means 'what is that?' God never told them what it was, except that this mysterious 'thing' was to be their desert food – their viatecum (food for the way) – until they reached the Promised Land. It was like coriander seed, white in colour, and resembled wafers made with honey (v.31).

It had mysterious properties. First: even though some gathered more, and some less, everyone discovered that he had just as much as he needed (vv.15–18). Second: if anyone disobeyed Moses in collecting enough for the following day, he found that it deteriorated and bred maggots so that he could not use it, so there was no advantage in being selfish – it automatically adapted to *needs* only (vv.19–21). Third: on the sixth day (Friday) they were allowed to gather a double portion – enough to last them on the Sabbath, and when they acted in obedience to the Lord's command, the manna did not deteriorate or breed maggots. If this were a purely 'natural' event how could this happen every Friday for forty years? Fourth: the manna ceased on the day they set foot in the Promised Land (v.35; Joshua 5:12). Fifth: the manna did not satisfy greed or any bodily craving; this was to become a problem later on in the journey (Numbers 11:6, 21:5). Sixth: manna – which could deteriorate and smell foul in one day

147

– was preserved successfully in a jar, which was later put into the Ark of the Covenant with the tablets of stone to remind the people of God's wonderful intervention on their behalf (16:12–14; Hebrews 9:4). By the time Solomon built the Temple and placed the Ark in the Holy of Holies the jar of manna had vanished; nowhere are we told what happened to it. Its disappearance is as mysterious as its arrival (cf. 1 Kings 8:9).

Manna contains a very deep message for God's children in every generation and it prepared the way for the revelation of Jesus to us. In the miracle of the manna and the water from the rock the Lord was telling His people that He was their very life and that He alone could sustain life in them. He wanted to be their food and drink! If we allow it, He will be our unfailing supply in every need; but unfortunately our independence rebels against this and we do not allow Him to be for us all that He wants to be. We block Him.

The manna typifies the spiritual nourishment that is essential for a successful journey through the wilderness. Our spiritual food consists of a three-part diet – the Eucharist, the Word of God and prayer – and the manna points to all three, showing how rich in depth of revelation were the signs that God gave to Israel.

Manna points to the Eucharist

Manna was a gift from God, bread from Heaven. Jesus claimed to be the fulfilment of this. 'It was *not* Moses who gave you the bread from heaven,' He said. 'It was my Father, and *this* bread gives life to the world' (John 6:33). '*I am* the bread of Life' (John 6:35). Jesus said that He alone could satisfy our hunger and thirst (6:36); He said, 'I am the bread that came down from Heaven' (John 6:41). The Manna was food they did not have to work for; they just had to pick it up and eat it to have as much as they needed. So too with the Eucharist which Jesus has made readily available for us each day, with no work on our part.

148

We just take and eat and it nourishes our souls.

Manna was small, fine and white, resembling the consecrated host, its whiteness denoting the purity of God's gift of love to us; with the Eucharist as with manna it is food for one day only. We can see that the faith of some Christians is dying because they do not feed on the Bread of Life frequently. To have a lively, growing relationship with the Lord it is good to feed on Him often, each day if possible. Take, for example, the image of a family sitting around the dinner table on Sunday. The father announces to his hungry growing children, 'Eat up now, there will be no more food until next Sunday!' The children could not possibly assimilate enough food in one meal to nourish them for a whole week! It is equally hard to grow fully in the spiritual life if we are nourished by the Eucharist only once a week. Fasting from our Divine Food puts a strain on our spiritual life. No wonder we fail the Lord so much!

Manna adapted itself to the needs of each person eating it. Some took more, some less, but they all got what they needed. So too with the Eucharist. Some feed more deeply on the Eucharist than others, even though all receive the same gift from Jesus. Many of the saints nourished themselves so deeply on the Eucharist that they needed very little food, or none – Catherine of Siena, Therese Neuman, Padre Pio.

According to our faith we can drink deeply from the well of salvation (Isaiah 12), but no one has ever or will ever drink the well dry! There is a plentiful supply for all hungry and thirsty souls.

Manna was a mystery to all the Israelites and incomprehensible to those lacking in faith, as is the mystery of the Eucharist. No matter how close to God the saint is he must bow before this wonderful mystery of Christ's love. But those whose faith is weak look at the Eucharist and say, 'What *is* it? It must be only a symbol, a remembrance. It couldn't be Jesus feeding us with His own Body and Blood'! And they walk away 'sick of this unsatisfying food' (Numbers 21:5) because they are unable to bow before the humility of a God who loves us to such a heroic degree! And they are unable to take into themselves this nourishment they need so badly. They remind one of children suffering from starvation, who are unable to eat when food is eventually put before them. But to walk away from the Bread of Life is frightening! The slow death of the body from starvation cannot be compared to the deprivation of the soul left without its spiritual food (cf. 1 Corinthians 11:28–32).

Manna remained a mystery to the pilgrims in the desert, but they took it, out of obedience to God. It was several hundred years later, when the full realization of what manna really was came to them, that they wrote 'You gave them the food of angels, from heaven untiringly sending them bread already prepared, containing every delight, satisfying every taste. And the substance you gave demonstrated your sweetness towards your children, for, conforming to the taste of whoever ate it, it transformed itself into what each eater wished' (Wisdom 16:20–21). Only later in their history did they realize that God fed body and soul with this mysterious food (Psalm 78:24–25). Those whose faith was deep enough really to assimilate this gift of God found that it *was* satisfying food. Only the unbelievers found it otherwise. So too with the Eucharist, which is nourishing soul food to the believer and incomprehensible to the unbeliever (cf. 1 Corinthians 2:14–16).

Manna points to the Word of God as food
One of the great lessons of the wilderness is that 'man does not live on bread alone, but on every word that comes from the mouth of God' (Deuteronomy 8:3; Matthew 4:4; Luke 4:4). The second source of spiritual food is the Word of God (scripture). As soon as the people began their journey God gave them His commands – even before the Covenant at Sinai. The true disciple is the one who does the will of God (Luke 8:21; Mark 3:35). Hence we must feed on

God's Word in scripture, a plentiful supply of food just as the manna was. It, too, is 'bread' from heaven on which the soul must feed each day, taking as much as it needs for growth. Like manna it is a gift of God, a mixture of the human and divine, and is incomprehensible to the unbeliever. The person whose spiritual life is growing finds it a mystery, but can nourish his soul on it with ever deepening relish – for it, too, conforms to the taste of each one! We need only to feed on the scriptures during our earthly pilgrimage as the Israelites fed only on manna. When we see the Lord face to face we will know even as we are known! (1 Corinthians 13:12). When we feed daily on our rich diet of Word and Bread then we grow steadily in the Lord's ways.

Manna points to Jesus, the incarnate Word

Like manna Jesus came down from Heaven to be our spiritual nourishment – not because of any good He found in His people, but just because of His own merciful love. He came to help us during our earthly pilgrimage through the wilderness of this world, so that we would never be alone or die from lack of help. As with the manna, we can feed on Jesus as our source of life as much as we wish. Some enter more deeply, some less into the life-giving relationship with Him in prayer and draw life from Him in greater or lesser degrees – but He is available for everyone to take as much as he needs. If the manna was a manifestation of the glory of God (16:7) how much more true it is that the incarnation of Jesus the Son of God was the *full* manifestation of that glory in our midst (John 1:14; Hebrews 1:3; 2 Peter 1:16–18). While manna was available for all, yet it was the responsibility of each individual to go out and collect his day's portion; so too, while Jesus the saviour came for all men, each one of us must enter into relationship with Him as an individual and appropriate His life and grace to ourselves so that we can benefit from the gift of our saviour, so that *the* Lord becomes *my* Lord, and *the* saviour becomes *my* saviour; then I experience in my own personal life all that this means (Romans 1:16; Mark 16:16; Galatians 2:20). The manna was a mystery to everyone and despised and rejected by some (Numbers 11:4–6, 21:5), just as the mystery of Christ, crucified and risen, has always been and is also today, a stumbling block and a scandal (cf. 1 Corinthians 1:17–25) to those without faith and to those who want to bring the mysteries of our faith down to a level the intellect can grasp and hold. But to those who enter deeply into the personal relationship with Jesus and allow His transforming grace to do its work in their souls, to these people this food of Heaven – Eucharist, scripture and the personal relationship with Jesus in prayer – is indeed the bread of angels adapting itself to every need and every taste, feeding us until we are hungry and thirsty no more (John 6:35), for we are filled with the utter fullness of God (Ephesians 3:19).

What a marvellous revelation was and is given through that tiny white thing – in the wilderness manna, but on our altars, the Eucharist. Let us never again say, 'What is it?' for we have tasted, we have seen and we *know* that it is the bread from Heaven. But the mystery for us is way beyond what the manna could signify, for we are not just fed on the Bread of Angels but on the sacred body and blood of Jesus Himself. We are fed on God Himself! And this food is so holy, so pure, so incredible a mystery of God's love that it is no wonder that it is incomprehensible to those lacking in faith or understanding. It is frightening today to see so many Christians look on, uncomprehending, at this manifestation of the glory of God in our midst. So many of them try to go on their pilgrim journey without this nourishment, so we must not be surprised to see them go astray from the path and faint on the way. How can they resist and overcome temptations and the inevitable weaknesses of the flesh when they refuse to be strengthened by the bread of the strong?

If we do not want to die in the wilderness or lose our way we should feed daily on this three-part spiritual diet which

gives us all the strength and guidance we need for the way.
There is no need for any of us to hear that awful censure
of the Lord given so often to the Israelites: 'If only you
would listen to Him today; do not harden your hearts'
. . . 'Don't have me say to *you* "How unreliable these
people are who *refuse* to grasp my ways"' (Psalm 95:8–11).

9. God Is Our Rock

Exodus 17:1–7

The revelation of the manna was an important point in the spiritual growth of the people. God expected them to continue to draw life from this food without complaint. New stages of growth awaited them, and deeper revelations of the Lord (v.1). From the wilderness of Sin they moved to Dophtek, and then to Alush, and on to encamp at Rephidim, where we encounter the next trial (cf. Numbers 33:12–15). There was no water here, but as they had suffered lack of water before (cf. 15:22) one would expect that they could handle it. Humble prayer to the Lord, who wanted to supply their every need, is all that was required. But no! They fell into the same disaster as before by keeping their eyes on the problem instead of on the Lord. Therefore we see them – yet again! – suffering tension, frustration, failure and sin! But let us be sympathetic, for they were 'tormented by thirst' (v.3). The dreadful thirst of a dry hot desert can leave a person crazed and unable to think. It was another test of faith and trust in the Lord – all the greater as they felt the wilderness close in on them, cutting off all possibility of their running back to the sea. Oh! it had been so easy to believe at the Red Sea, but now, deprived of everything, apparently going nowhere and achieving nothing, it was a different matter! Even Egypt seemed better than this (v.3) (cf. Numbers 20:5). Their anger reached such a pitch they were ready to stone Moses – their liberator – to death (vv. 4–5).

They had forgotten a vital point, it was the Lord who had brought them here, guiding them step by step with the pillar of Cloud and Fire (Exodus 40:36–38). He had not done this to torment them but to show them constant proofs of His powerful loving presence – if only they would turn to Him and ask! 'Ask and it will be given to you . . . anything you ask for in prayer you will receive if you have faith [trust]' (Matthew 7:7, 21:22). But God is always the last person we turn to in our need.

Moses prayed for them and the Lord instructed him to stand before the people with some of the elders, holding the staff of God in his hand. There before their eyes he was to strike the rock, and God would provide a plentiful supply of water for His thirsty people (vv. 4–5).

What does the rock signify? God had said, 'I will be standing before you there on the rock . . .' (v.6). The Lord was offering Himself as the answer to the burning thirst of His people: 'Come to Me . . . I will give you rest!' (Matthew 11:28ff). The invitation to the Israelites was to come closer to Him and draw from *Him* the answer to all their needs. There was no criticism of their behaviour, just compassion and an invitation to closer intimacy. St Paul interprets this mystery for us: 'I want to remind you, brothers, how our fathers were all guided by a cloud above them and how they all passed through the sea. They were all baptized into Moses in this cloud and in this sea; all ate the same spiritual food and . . . all drank from the *spiritual rock that followed them as they went, and that rock was Christ*' (1 Corinthians 10:1–40). St Paul here alludes to an ancient tradition which held that this 'rock' accompanied the Israelites on their journey (2 Samuel 22:2–3; Psalm 18:2, 31, 46). Jewish commentators tended to identify it with the Lord Himself, hence scripture abounds with references to 'the Lord my rock', 'He is the rock' (Deuteronomy 32:4), '. . . the rock of his salvation (Deuteronomy 32:15), '. . . the rock who begot you, the God who fathered you' (Deuteronomy 32:18), '. . . my rock, my safety' (Psalm 62:5–7), '. . . the rock of rest and refreshment . . .' (Isaiah 32:2). Not only are we told here in Exodus that water came from the rock; later we hear of fire from the rock (Judges 6:21), honey from the rock (Psalm 81:16) and oil from the rock

(Deuteronomy 32:13). This 'rock' was the source of life, joy, refreshment and strength – it was the Lord revealing Himself as the source of all good. Jesus claimed to be the fulfilment of this mystery when He cried out:

> 'If any man is thirsty, let him come to me!
> Let the man come and drink who believes in me!'
> As scripture says, From his breast shall flow
> fountains of living water.

> (John 7:37–38)

Jesus, therefore, is the rock of our salvation who had to be 'struck' so that the living waters of divine life would flow abundantly for all thirsty souls (John 19:34). He abides in our hearts – the 'rock' travelling with us – as the answer to our daily needs. The smiting of the rock therefore points to the death of Jesus as the source of divine life. It is significant that it was the sins of the people that led to this manifestation of God's love, and the sins of the world that necessitated the death of Jesus for our salvation. As Isaiah so rightly said, 'He was pierced through for our sins' (Isaiah 53:4–5).

The flow of water from the rock also points to the outpouring of the Holy Spirit after the death and Resurrection of Jesus. St John continues from the passage above: 'He was speaking of the Spirit which those who believed in Him were to receive; for there was no Spirit as yet because Jesus had not yet been glorified' (John 7:39). Just as the water from the Rock was for everyone, so the Holy Spirit was to be poured out on all flesh (Joel 3:1–3).

Moses called this place Masah (trial) and Meribah (contention) because the people had put God to the test, saying, 'Is the Lord with us or not?' (vv.2,7) and because of their contention with Moses. Here we see again how God responded to the sinfulness of the people with incredible goodness.

Spiritual warfare (17:8–16)

It was at Rephidim that Israel had her first taste of war. The Israelites had been protected until now because God saw they were too young in the spirit and might lose heart (cf. 13:17). He never tries us beyond our strength. But now that the Lord was their rock, their fortress (Psalm 104), their salvation, they were given a small taste of battle, even though they were ill-equipped and undisciplined. The battle itself would alert them to put order into their lives. Here, too, just when they needed him, we are introduced to Joshua, who was appointed army commander by Moses and who was destined to succeed Moses as leader and take the people into the Promised Land.

If we reflect that the striking of the rock points to the death of Jesus and the flow of water to the outpouring of the Holy Spirit, then we see how well placed this incident is in the sacred text. The gospels show us that the Apostles were protected by Jesus from the hatred and opposition of the 'world' and the authorities before His death, but after Pentecost, when they had been filled and strengthened by the outpouring of the Holy Spirit, we find them engaged in spiritual warfare with those in authority, with the 'world' and with evil in others (cf. Acts 4:5, 13:6–12, 16:16–18, etc.).

Nevertheless, the spiritual struggle is two-sided. We engage in conflict as we continue the mission of Jesus in a sinful world; we must also face the struggle with our own corrupt nature. The flesh wars against the spirit in us (Galatians 5:16–17), so if we are to grow to spiritual maturity we must crucify (ban) all self-indulgent passions and desires (Galatians 5:24). The struggle is not easy (Romans 7) but we shall see here how to gain the victory.

It was Amalek who made war on Israel, not vice versa. It is the 'old man' in us that struggles against the spirit. God allows circumstances to overtake us, to show up the need for us to fight the good fight. We have to learn how to deal with these circumstances. Moses ordered Joshua to march out and engage Amalek in battle while he, with Aaron and Hur, was to position himself on a nearby hilltop to fight the battle in prayer, holding the Staff of God in his hand (v.10).

The first lesson then is to face a problem – but never in your own strength. The battle must be fought and won in prayer also. It is there that the strengthening grace is given to persevere on to victory. Without this the battle would be lost (v.11). The actions of Joshua and Moses were closely linked, as we see from the fact that Joshua lost the advantage to Amalek whenever Moses grew tired and let his arms drop. They won the day because Aaron and Hur supported Moses' arms until sunset (vv.11–14; cf. 1 Timothy 2:8). Many fail miserably in the fight against the flesh because they either do not pray at all or pray enough (cf. James 4:3). Jesus counselled us to pray continually without losing heart (Luke 18:1). The young Church took this literally, and the Acts show her members continually in prayer for strength to deal with the struggles involved in the apostolate (cf. Acts 1:14, 2:42, 4:24–31).

Moses was not alone in prayer. He was helped by Aaron the High Priest and Hur (which means light). We too are not left to ourselves in prayer. Jesus, our High Priest, ever lives to make intercession for us (Hebrews 7:25), and the Holy Spirit comes to help our weakness and prays within us according to God's will (Romans 8:26–27).

The second lesson here is that the enemy was put to flight, not by prayer alone, but by prayer and the sword (vv.13, 15, 17:45). The sword points to the Word of God – called the 'sword of the Spirit' (Ephesians 6:17) – which we must use daily in our spiritual battles. Jesus set the example for us in His spiritual struggle with Satan in the wilderness (Matthew 4:1–11 and Luke 4:1–13), when He defended Himself with the scriptures. Like Him we will prevail in all our struggles against evil within ourselves, and outside of us, if we are armed with the Sword of God and a deep prayer life.

The final words in this passage are important. Moses was instructed by God to record this event in writing. The people were told to remember the lessons the Lord taught them, for future generations would need them. Now they knew that He was not only their rock but their banner and their safety in battle. They built an altar to God, called *Yahweh Nissi* – 'the Lord is our banner' (v.16). They would need to remember this, for war with the Amalekites had just begun and would continue until King David defeated them (v.16; cf. 1 Samuel 30; 2 Samuel 1:1).

The same applies to us. Spiritual warfare continues until we either give up and settle for mediocrity or fight on to complete victory (cf. Philippians 3:21). If we persevere we too, like Moses, will know it was not Joshua who won the victory but the Lord, and we will proclaim that it was achieved through grace.

The events dealt with here break the chronological order of the book, for they deal with incidents which occurred when Israel was about to depart from Sinai for the wilderness of Paran, whereas chapter 17 had the people at Rephidim and chapter 19 at Sinai (Horeb) (cf. Deuteronomy 1:6–18). Jethro, Moses' father-in-law, came to meet Moses, for news had reached him concerning all the wonders the Lord had done for Israel. He brought with him Zipporah, Moses' wife, and her two sons. Moses had dismissed her – apparently before returning to Egypt. Her refusal to circumcise her son may have been the cause (cf. 4:24–26), for this would amount to a refusal to recognize the Lord had come under His Covenant. She and her children were restored to Moses when he was at the height of his glory (vv.2–7). Some take this to signify that the nation of Israel will be restored to God when she accepts her Messiah coming in glory. Then the scandal of the cross will have been removed for Israel, and she will no longer turn away from Christ's sacrifice on Calvary. If this is so, then the names of her two sons, Gershom – 'a stranger' – and Eliezer – 'God is my help' – would indicate that during all the years of her worldwide dispersion God never abandoned her, but instead preserved her from being either annihilated or assimilated among the Gentiles. God is faithful even if Israel, His chosen spouse, is unfaithful.

The seventy elders (18:1–27)

Jethro, rejoicing in the Lord's love for Israel, offered sacrifice, acknowledging the Lord to be greater than all the gods (vv.9–12). Moses, Aaron and the elders shared this sacrificial meal together.

Before leaving for Midian, Jethro advised Moses to delegate authority among the elders of Israel. It was too great a burden for him to administer all civil, legal and religious matters alone (vv. 13–18). It would be better for him to teach and guide the people but to leave smaller matters of administration and disputes to other trustworthy leaders (vv.19–21). Moses appointed seventy judges over the people, which freed him to deal with the spiritual leadership. Both Numbers 11:14 and Deuteronomy 1:9–18 show Moses taking this decision without Jethro's intervention, but the people agreed to the new leaders (Deuteronomy 1:14). God instructed Moses to take the seventy elders before Him at the Tent of Meeting; He would take some of the spirit that was upon Moses and share it among them. This would empower them for their task of administering the people (cf. Numbers 11:16–30). The leadership rested with Moses; the elders merely shared in it. The Lord offered no fresh anointing.

IV. The Time of Consecration

10. Glory on the Mountain

The fundamental element behind the whole process of salvation is the fact that God wants to draw us into intimacy of union with Himself. Chapters 1–15 of Exodus demonstrate what Israel was saved *from*; now we are to observe what they were saved *for*. The people had learned much about the Lord, for they had witnessed His judgements on Pharaoh and Egypt, His power at the Red Sea and His wonderful provision in the wilderness. Their greatest privilege was yet to come. They knew now that the Lord was the sovereign Lord of the universe, and Lord of history, the only True God, whose word could be trusted absolutely. He was waiting for them on Sinai where He would show them His glory and majesty. It was the appointed place and time for them to consecrate themselves to Him and become His own unique people for all time. Through them He would set up a theocratic nation – the Kingdom of God. Their commitment would be ratified in a solemn Covenant, and then God would give to them the promise of Abraham – the Promised Land. Chapters 19–24 deal with the event that made this people so special, namely the Sinaitic Covenant.

An appointment with God (Exodus 19:1–15)
Three months after the departure from Egypt Israel left Rephidim, moved into the wilderness of Sinai and pitched

camp before the holy mountain (vv.1–2). The location of this place is said to be Jebel Musa – the mountain of Moses – in the south of the Sinai Peninsula. Thus was fulfilled God's promise to Moses: 'After you have led the people out of Egypt, you are to offer worship to God on this mountain' (cf. 3:12). Here we see that all the wonders that accompanied the exodus from Egypt were designed to enable the people to keep their appointment with God on Sinai.

Moses ascended the mountain alone, and was instructed by God to remind the people of all that He had done for them, and to propose that they enter into Covenant with Him. He had borne with them gently, like a mother eagle caring for her young, and now He had brought them to Himself (vv.3–4). How beautifully He passed over their sinfulness and lack of trust! All that is forgotten now that they have arrived at Sinai. If they would agree to the terms of the Covenant, He would choose them – out of all nations – to be His own special people, and make them into a kingdom of priests and a nation consecrated to – or set apart for – God (v.5). Moses descended the mountain, placed God's incredible offer before the people and the elders, and it met with unanimous approval: 'All that the Lord has said we will do' (v.8). Moses, the mediator, took the people's reply back to God.

The moment had come which would give new meaning to Israel's existence and determine her destiny. The Lord and Israel had agreed to bind each other by a legal contract constituting Him as King of Israel and the people as His subjects (Deuteronomy 4:20). The people have now become a nation and the Lord, as Lawgiver, will give them His Laws in the Torah – the Decalogue and the Book of the Covenant. There would be great blessings for those who observed the Covenant, and great affliction for those who broke it. It was the most solemn pact that could be made.

The preparation (19:9–15)

Two days were set aside for preparation, in which they purified themselves, washed their clothes and abstained from sexual relations. The Lord had made it clear at Sinai before (3:1–6) that He was coming as a God of holiness, who would require a response of reverence and holiness from His people. To wash one's clothes was a traditional gesture expressing the need for purity in anyone who would approach God (cf. Genesis 35:2; Leviticus 11:25, etc.). Marital abstinence was obligatory, because sexual intercourse was believed to render a person unfit to enter God's presence (cf. Leviticus 15:17; 1 Samuel 21:4–5). Finally, to express the gulf which exists between the All-Holy God and sinful man, barriers were erected around the mountain to keep the people at a safe distance (vv.12–13). The penalty for trespassing on the holy ground was death, and the offender would be stoned or shot with arrows, for the executioner would also incur death if he entered the sacred space! (v.13; cf. 3:5).

Our God reigns (19:16–25)

The Lord kept His promise. At daybreak on the third day He began to manifest Himself in glory and majesty, as the Lord of the storm. Thunder and lightning drew the people's attention to the mountain, just as the burning bush had earlier attracted Moses. A dense cloud descended, indicating the approach of God, which was also heralded by a loud trumpet blast (v.16). The people trembled in fear as Moses led them out of the camp to meet God. They stood in reverential fear and awesome silence as the greatest moment in their history approached. The people, as a whole, were to see God – and live! Since the fall of Adam God had manifested Himself only to a chosen few – Abraham, Isaac, Jacob, Joseph and Moses – but now, for once only in their history, all Israel would see God.

They could never again say that they knew Him just on the word of another (cf. John 4:42). They knew Him personally in a new way, for they had seen Him, the One to whom they had consecrated themselves. The gospels show us one moment of glory for the Apostles too – on Mount Tabor, when they beheld the divinity in Jesus and heard the voice of God speak to them. For the rest of their lives (apart from the Resurrection appearances) they were to move in the darkness of faith, as all of God's servants must do both in the Old and New Covenants (Testaments).

The Lord descended on the mountain in the form of fire, while the mountain was wrapped in smoke and shook violently (v.18). Moses conversed with God, whose voice sounded like peals of thunder (cf. John 12:28–29). Invited to enter more deeply into the divine presence, Moses was again warned to maintain the sacred distance between the people and God, but an exception was made of Aaron, the High Priest (vv.20–25).

The descent of the Holy Spirit on the Church at Pentecost was similar to this. It seemed as if a powerful wind storm entered the room where the Apostles and Mary awaited the promise of Jesus in prayer (Acts 1:4, 2:1–13). Their preparation was an interior one lasting nine days before the glory of God broke in upon them. The Holy Spirit came in the form of fire, just as the Lord did on Sinai, but with this essential difference: there was no barrier – no distance – to be kept before Him. He entered into each one of them filling them – internally – with His presence, power and love until they were drunk with the glory of God (Acts 2:12–13). Thus we see that Pentecost far surpassed Sinai as a visitation of God. Sinai was an external manifestation followed by external ceremonial laws of worship, but at Pentecost each person was drawn into an awesome intimacy with God, where he would henceforth worship Him in spirit and in truth (John 4:24).

The people were terrified of God and begged Moses to act as mediator on their behalf. God had wanted to confirm Moses as mediator and lawgiver (19:9), as well as to establish His Covenant among them. How different from Pentecost, where perfect love cast out all fear (1 John 4:18). Pentecost was the love of God poured forth into our hearts, but Sinai was to establish the reverential fear of God which would prevent the people from sinning (v.20). Only the mediator could enter into the dark cloud of God's presence – the people stayed at a distance (v.21).

Moses interpreted this experience for them at a later date (Deuteronomy 5:23–31), declaring that God had shown them His glory and greatness and that they had truly heard His voice from the heart of the fire. The purpose was to instil the fear of God into them, to motivate them to keep His commandments. The discipline of Law (Sinai) was the necessary preparation for the manifestation of Love (Pentecost), but obedience to God's will and commandments was the acceptable *sign* of love from God's people in both Testaments. The obligations that the people were undertaking in the Covenant were very serious. This manifestation of God's holiness would prevent them from taking it lightly. The fear of God would guide them to wisdom and right moral judgements (Psalm 111:10, 119:38; Proverbs 8:13, 14:27).

The Covenant ratified (24:1–11)
The insertion of the Law in the text from chapters 20–23 interrupts the narration of events on Sinai, because the authors want us to grasp that the Torah (Law) was given by God on Sinai in consequence of the Covenant. Here we shall deal with the ratification of the Covenant before handling the Law.

We have now reached the highest peak of the Old Testament – the moment when Moses, as Mediator, was permitted to take Aaron, his two sons Nadab and Abihu and the seventy elders into the august presence of God. All except Moses were to worship at a distance; this showed that sinful man gains access to God only through the Covenant (vv. 1–2). Moses here points to Christ, who alone has access to God, and through whom we all gain access on the grounds of the New Covenant sealed in His own blood for us (cf. Hebrews 9:11–28; 1 Peter 3:18). Returning to the people, Moses proclaimed God's Law (chapters 20–23), showing them clearly what they were binding themselves to. Again they unanimously consented to proceed, and Moses committed the Law to writing (probably at a later date!) in order to perpetuate it for their descendants and as a witness for them (vv.3–4). He then built an altar at the foot of the mountain with twelve stones (or pillars) representing the twelve tribes who entered into the Covenant. He then directed some of the young men to offer sacrifices to the Lord. These young men – probably heads of families or the redeemed firstborn – were chosen because the official priesthood was not yet formed. These were communion sacrifices or peace offerings that were associated with feasts; this was the feast they had been invited to while still in Egypt (Leviticus 3:1–17; cf. Exodus 5:2). The slaughtered animal was divided up, part being burnt on the altar as an offering to God, and part eaten as a communion meal, expressing the union now existing between the people and God. They were one in this Covenant bond – 'blood brothers'. The blood of the animal, which was considered very special, was collected in basins. Moses took half the blood and poured it on the altar, thus binding the Lord to His side of the contract. Then he read the Book of the Covenant (v.7, chapters 20–23) to the people, who affirmed their consent to obey God's Law again. Then Moses solemnly sprinkled some of the blood over the people, declaring that it was the blood of the Covenant which legally bound them to the Lord according to the laws of the Covenant (v.8). The pact was now sealed and permanent. Israel could no longer be understood apart from her special relationship to God. Her moral and spiritual life must be evaluated against this solemn contract with God on Sinai. Her marriage to the Lord was signed and sealed, and henceforth her prophets would speak to her in terms of fidelity to her marriage vows (cf. Hosea, chapter 2).

Moses, Aaron and the elders then went up the mountain to meet God. The 'then' is important (v.9). It was *after* the ratification of the Covenant and the sprinkling of the blood that they could approach the All-Holy God. As the representatives of His Covenanted people they could enjoy His glory and have communion with Him (vv.10–11). Because of this they did not incur the death penalty; instead, they ate and drank in His presence.

The indescribable happened – they gazed on the Lord, the God of Israel; but they saw no shape, no form, as Deuteronomy 4:12 tells us. They described the pavement under 'His feet' like a sapphire as pure as the heavens. Among the few who have been gifted with such an exalted vision we find the prophet Ezekiel, and St John the Evangelist. Both use language very similar to that of Moses. Ezekiel described God's voice like that of a storm, and His throne was made of sapphire (Ezekiel 1:26), while John said the voice of God was like a trumpet; he saw flashes of lightning and heard peals of thunder coming from the throne (Revelation 4:1, 5). Both describe God as 'Light' (cf. Ezekiel 1:28; see also Isaiah 6:1–4). This must be the only language available to men in describing the ineffable glory of the Lord.

Moses on the mountain (24:12–18)
God invited Moses to ascend the top of the mountain where, as mediator, he would be given the tables of the Law. The people were to receive the Decalogue and the Book of the Covenant as their rule of life. The Cloud, indicating God's presence, covered the mountain, and the glory of the Lord – the Shekinah – settled on Sinai. To the eyes of the people at the foot of the mountain the Shekinah looked like a devouring fire on the mountain top – hence they said afterwards, 'our God is a consuming fire' (cf. Deuteronomy 4:24; Hebrews 12:29). Moses took Joshua with him part of the way, because he was now being trained

to take over the leadership from Moses. They waited six days. Six is the number of man, indicating imperfection and man's destitution and hopelessness without God, but seven is the number of perfection and the completeness of God's work. It was on the seventh day that Moses was called to enter into the cloud, and stayed there for forty days and forty nights (v.18). Forty is a very significant number in scripture; it does not necessarily denote six weeks but a particular period of preparation in which God can manifest something new in the economy of salvation. It is closely connected with Moses as redeemer and mediator; he underwent forty years of preparation in the house of Pharaoh, then forty years in the wilderness, prior to the revelation of his mission before the Burning Bush. He was now in a forty-year process of preparing the people for the Promised Land and, within this, undergoing a forty-day preparation to receive the Torah from the hand of God. Jesus, too, had a forty-day trial in the wilderness to prepare Him for His mission as Messiah. His life may have been forty years long in preparation for the full glory of redemption in His 'hour'. This was followed by a forty-day revelation after Easter to prepare for Ascension and Pentecost.

Moses' sojourn on the Mount points to the Ascension and the glorification of Jesus after He had sealed the New Covenant in His own blood for us. The six days here then would indicate His labours in redemption before entering His sabbath rest on the seventh day (cf. Hebrews 3:7–4:11). As St John puts it: 'I have glorified you on earth and finished the work that you have given me to do. Now, Father, it is time for you to glorify me with that glory I had with you before ever the world was made' (John 17:4–5).

During his stay Moses received from the Lord the revelation concerning the Tabernacle, which fills the next seven chapters of Exodus (chapters 25–31). This taught the people how to avail themselves of the treasures God was offering through the Covenant of His chosen people (cf. Exodus 25:40; Hebrews 8:5).

The nature of Covenant

Arriving at Sinai we reach a landmark, not only in the history of Israel, but also in the history of religion, for here a revealed religion with laws, liturgy and hierarchy became historical fact for the first time. God revealed it to Moses, who transmitted it to the people. Eventually it was committed to writing under the inspiration of the Holy Spirit, so that it became 'scripture', or God's revealed Word for all mankind. Now, at last, God had made known His will and His children must abide by it.

In communicating His will (Law) to us God had to adapt Himself to our way of thinking so that divine truth could be expressed in ways which we could grasp. He had to move from the natural, which we know, to the supernatural, which is unknown to us. God had to come down to the level of His creatures, in the same way as a mother will do for a child, and make use of our human institutions, laws and customs, while transforming them by His Living Truth.

From the beginning God dealt with mankind through Covenants – also called treaties or pacts – which already existed. These were legal contracts which bound individuals or nations to mutually agreed obligations; examples are the pact between Abraham and Abimelech over the ownership of a well (Genesis 21:22–32), and the marriage agreement between Jacob and Laban (Genesis 31:43–56). When God made Covenants with Noah, Abraham and Moses, therefore, He made use of a very ancient custom which the people concerned understood. Sacrifice would accompany the making of a covenant.

God made Covenants with His creatures in order to unite them to Himself and establish the Kingdom of God on earth. The first one was made with Adam, God promising him immortality, integrity and paradise, but it was conditional on Adam's obeying one law which was given to test his obedience. The breaking of this Covenant incurred the penalty of death and exclusion from paradise. The broken relationship between God and man was to be restored very gradually, beginning with the Covenants with Noah and Abraham, then more fully at Sinai. It would be completed with the redemption wrought by Jesus on Calvary.

The process of restoration began when God made a covenant with Noah (Genesis 9:8–17) which included all creatures. It was unconditional because He imposed no law on mankind. He established the rainbow as the sign of His Covenant fidelity. Next came the Covenant with Abraham (Genesis 15:17), which was renewed under Isaac and Jacob. Here God promised Abraham posterity and a homeland in Palestine, with blessing for all mankind through him (Genesis 12:3, 15:5–6). For his part Abraham would have to serve God with integrity, and trust in the promise (Genesis 15:6; Romans 4:1–25). Circumcision was the external sign of the Covenant, cut in his own body. As no law was imposed this was an unconditional Covenant, just as it was eternal because no time limit was set. It found fulfilment and perfection in the New Testament (cf. Luke 1:55–73). It was according to this Covenant that God dealt with the Israelites during the exodus from Egypt to Sinai. His changed attitude towards them after Sinai was due to the conditional Covenant they had agreed to enter into with Him. He dealt with them according to their sworn commitment to abide by His Law.

The Sinaitic Covenant was bilateral: God extended the promise of Abraham to include the whole nation – his posterity. For their part they would put their faith in the promise and abide by the Mosaic Law. The extraordinary privilege of this Covenant lay in the fact that the nation of Israel was now God's chosen people; He now dwelt among them in the Tabernacle above the Ark of the Covenant, and for the first time they had the scriptures, in the Torah.

This pact with God resembles the so-called Suzerainty treaties made between kings and their vassals in the ancient world. They began by identifying the covenanting king, giving his titles and attributes (Exodus 20:1–2): 'I am the Lord, your God'. The king's benevolence to his subjects is then related: '. . . who brought you out of the house of bondage.' The list of laws imposed by the king follows – see the Ten Commandments: 20:3–17. These regulate relationships between the king and his subjects, and also between individuals in the nation. As subjects they were to present themselves to the king once yearly to pay tribute: Exodus 23:17 expects the men to present themselves to the Lord three times a year. They were to submit difficult disputes to the king (cf. Deuteronomy 17:8–13). The Covenant would be written, deposited in the Temple and read periodically (cf. Deuteronomy 10:5, 31:9–13). A list of witnesses was normally included, which in pagan lands was a list of their gods. Deuteronomy 32:1 and Isaiah 1:2 call the heavens to witness against the infidelity of Israel (cf. Joshua 24:22–23). Finally the Covenant included a list of blessings and curses for those who kept or broke the sacred pact (cf. Deuteronomy 27, 28).

From this it would seem that Moses adapted a well-known form of contract to express the new relationship and status that existed between the Lord and Israel. *How* Israel reached her new status is not nearly as important as the fact that, as a result of this Covenant, she became a consecrated nation, a people set apart for God, a theocratic nation. God Himself was King, Lawgiver and Judge; but He exercised His Rule through representatives: Moses at first, later the judges and later still through prophets, priests and kings. The situation continued until the sceptre passed to Him to whom it belonged, namely Jesus Christ (cf. 1 Corinthians 15:22–28; Ephesians 5:24–33; Hebrews 12:18–29). The Church-nation which was inaugurated on Sinai was to give way to the Church proper, which would have no national boundaries and would comprise the community of all those who believe, the true posterity of Abraham.

Towards the New Covenant

Israel did not remain faithful to the Lord for very long (cf. Exodus 32). Her weary history of infidelity began only weeks after her glorious experience on Sinai – before they had even moved camp! She seemed only to have grasped her privileged position before God (cf. Jeremiah 5:12; John 6:45–47, 8:33–42) and not the grave obligations it involved (Jeremiah 2:19), consequently her prophets and teachers down through the centuries challenged her to live what she professed, warning her about the catastrophes that would follow her breaches of the Covenant. They searched for images to explain her relationship with the Lord, with a view to motivating her to loving obedience: the Lord was the shepherd, Israel His flock; He the vinedresser, she the vine; the Lord was the father, with Israel as His firstborn son; He was her bridegroom and she His chosen bride. These images show that the loving obedience required of her came out of her relationship – it was not just a matter of Law. It came from the Lord's extraordinary election of Israel at Sinai (cf. Deuteronomy 4:37, 7:8, 10:15; Ezekiel 16:6–14), and love could be repaid by love alone (Deuteronomy 6:5, 10:12). The choice to love or not was a life and death matter for this people (Deuteronomy 30:15–20); hence, after her repeated infidelities, the Lord was forced to inflict the chastisements that followed the breaking of the Covenant, namely the destruction of Jerusalem, the exile and the dispersion of her people among the Gentiles as slaves again. This meant going back to 'square one' or cycle one (cf. Jeremiah 7:23–28, 11:1–14, 31:32; 2 Kings 17:7–23, etc.).

The sin and punishment of Israel was not to be the end of the road, for the Lord still considered *Himself* bound to Israel, and he could not allow the sinfulness of His people to prevent His loving designs for the redemption of the world from being fulfilled. Through the prophet Jeremiah

He promised a New Covenant which would be far superior to the Sinaitic Covenant, because the New Law would be written on our hearts (Jeremiah 31:31–34). God would pour out His Spirit on all flesh (Joel 3:1–3), touching and transforming our hearts, so that His grace would produce in us the interior response of attachment and obedience to His will (cf. Ezekiel 36:25–27). In this way God would succeed in setting up the Kingdom of God on earth through His faithful disciples.

The Covenant of Jesus

The gospels portray Jesus inaugurating the New Covenant at the Last Supper, where He consecrated the bread and wine of the Passover meal to become, by His divine power, His own body and blood. 'Take it and eat, this is my Body', He said. Then He took the cup of wine, blessed it and passed it to the disciples saying, 'This is my blood, *the blood of the covenant*, which will be shed for many' (Mark 14:24). Matthew adds 'for the remission of sins', and both Paul and Luke say, 'This is *the new covenant in my blood* which will be shed for you' (Luke 22:20; 1 Corinthians 11:25). Jesus, therefore, saw His death as the sacrifice for sin which would redeem the whole human race. His precious blood was poured over the Calvary altar and must be applied to the people for their salvation (Hebrews 9:23–28; 1 Peter 1:18–20). Jesus is not only the mediator of the New Covenant, but priest and victim also (Hebrews 3:1; John 3:29). Everything is accomplished in and through Him. Animal sacrifice is no longer acceptable to God, who has received the 'once-and-for-all' perfect sacrifice of Jesus (Hebrews 9:25–27), the Lamb of God. It is through this new sacrifice that union with God is established universally and eternally.

The Covenant theme is the background to the whole New Testament: Jesus is the fulfilment of the promise to Abraham (Genesis 3:15–18). The New Covenant is superior to the old (Sinaitic) because it offers the forgiveness of sins (Romans 11:27); it is written on our hearts (2 Corinthians 3:6), because God is with us (Emmanuel), indwelling us so that we are the temples of God (2 Corinthians 6:16). He has made us children in His family (Ephesians 4:24), and filled us with His Spirit (Romans 8:4–16); He has made us co-heirs with Christ, sharing in His suffering as well as sharing in His glory (Romans 8:17).

In the Letter to the Hebrews we see Jesus as the High Priest of all the blessings to come, entering the heavenly sanctuary to the Holy of Holies – the very throne of God, taking His own precious blood to plead our redemption, which is an eternal and universal redemption (Hebrews 9:11–12). The result is an inward purification of the heart enabling us to enter into union with God (v.14). Hebrews chapter 12 compares the two Covenants, contrasting the terror of Sinai with the joyful privilege of the Christian, where everyone is a firstborn son and a citizen of heaven. Jesus, the mediator of the New Covenant sealed in His own blood, brings God's work of redemption to its climax (Hebrews 12:18–24). Now, purified from our sins (Hebrews 9:14–22), we have access to God with confidence (Hebrews 10:19) and are constituted the New Israel, the new chosen people, a priestly people – the people of God (1 Peter 1:4–5, 9–10), a pilgrim people on our journey through history to the Promised Land in Heaven (1 Peter 1:11).

The Covenant and Eucharist
The Church teaches us that 'The renewal in the Eucharist of the Covenant between the Lord and man draws the faithful into the compelling love of Christ and sets them afire . . . from the Eucharist, as from a fountain, grace is channelled into us; and the sanctification of man in Christ and the glorification of God . . . are most powerfully achieved' (Constitution on the Liturgy, No. 10). Whenever we celebrate the Eucharist we share in the effects of

redemption 'Proclaiming the death of the Lord until He comes' (1 Corinthians 11:26). We participate in the communion meal, eating and drinking the Lord's flesh and blood, joyfully in His presence, just as the leaders ate and drank in God's presence on Sinai (24:11). Our invitation to share at His table proclaims that we are 'family' (Hebrews 3:6), for those outside the Covenant do not partake of the Covenant meal (1 Corinthians 10:16–17). At each Eucharistic celebration the Church proclaims God's Word to us, which continually reminds us of God's wonders to His people and of our obligation to keep His Commandments as His Covenanted people of today (cf. Joshua 24:3–34). Daily, on our altars, the once-and-for-all sacrifice of Jesus which ratified the New Covenant in His blood, is made present and effective for us, and we, as His Covenant community, express our allegiance to Him and His Law, and with Him intercede for the needs of the world. Unlike Moses, who could only remain in the divine presence a short time, Jesus, our mediator, intercedes for us at the throne of God effectively and for ever (Hebrews 7:25). Until He comes on the clouds of Heaven we continue to renew His Covenant and apply its grace to our lives, listening to, and obeying His Word 'as we wait in joyful hope' for the glorious fulfilment in the New Jerusalem (Revelation 21).

The Law

Both God and Jesus made the same request to their followers: 'If you love me, keep my commandments' (Exodus 15:26; John 14:21). The Decalogue – or Ten Words – is the unique expression of God's will that governs our relationship with Him and with each other. Obedience is the acceptable sign of love, and the gospels show the perfect obedience of Jesus, the Son, to His Heavenly Father: 'My food is to do the will of the one who sent me' (John 4:34); 'my aim is to do not my own will, but the will of him who sent me' (John 5:30); 'I faithfully keep His

Word' (John 8:55); '. . . . what I was to say, what I had to speak, was commanded by the Father who sent me, and I know that His commands mean eternal life. And therefore what the Father has told me is what I speak' (John 12:49–50); '. . . the world must be brought to know that I love the Father and that I am doing exactly what the Father told me' (John 14:31); 'It is accomplished' (John 19:30).

Since obedience to God's will was to be the sign of love, it is significant that the Lord waited until Sinai to reveal His Law. His people had to come *to know* Him first. Only after this could they love and serve Him. Obedience would become the ideal of love now that He had revealed His will (cf. Psalm 40:8; 1 John 5:2–3; Psalm 119:97). It was God's *love* that provided the Law which would guide His people to become a priestly, consecrated nation. This Law – properly called The Torah (meaning instruction) – consisted of the Decalogue and the Book of the Covenant.

Scripture speaks of three Laws – the Law of God, the Law of Moses and the Law of Christ, or the New Law. The Law of God refers to the Decalogue revealed by God on Sinai, which was written on tables of stone by the hand of God Himself (Exodus 32:16). These are binding on all humanity and form the basic moral code governing human behaviour. As the 'natural law' it was in operation from the beginning of creation. Cain was expected to obey it (Genesis 4:7). The Deluge was the final result of a whole people breaking from it (Genesis 6:5–7); and the Israelites were known as just or wicked according to its standards (Genesis 4:3–4, 5:24, 6:8–9, 6:5, 11f, etc.). At Sinai God crystallized it into ten words – the Ten Commandments.

The Law of Moses comprises the rest of the Mosaic Law, binding only on those governed by the Sinaitic Covenant (cf. Acts 15). It dealt with the ceremonial Law and the judicial system governing the people at that time.

The Law of Christ is the New Law promulgated by Jesus in the Sermon on the Mount. He did not abolish the Decalogue (Romans 7:25) but raised its standards to new spiritual heights (cf. Matthew 5:20–48). The old Law reached its fulfilment in the New (Matthew 5:17), and obedience to God's will remains the standard of perfection (cf. Ephesians 6:6).

The Decalogue: God's ten words (20:1–17)

God's first word of command set the tone for all the others: 'I am the Lord your God . . . you are to have no other gods before Me' (vv.1–3). This recognition of one God distinguished Israel from all other nations. Her experience of Him in the exodus led her to proclaim that He had no equal (15:11), and now He demands her exclusive worship. Never again can she put a creature, a 'thing' (an idol), before Him, for the Lord is 'no – *thing*'; He is a spirit that cannot be compared with anything or anyone (vv.4–5). Idols are nothing (i.e. have no existence) and insult the Living God (cf. Jeremiah 18:15). The contradiction is that these 'nothings' made of wood or stone seduced the people, who, because of their spiritual blindness, thought they represented reality. The Lord, the God of Israel, is the reality whom we are to worship as sovereign Lord of the universe and the creator of all things.

This commandment puts before *us* the clear choice between God and self. God is to have first place in our hearts and be the supreme authority in our lives. The breaking of this command consists in giving to a creature or a 'thing' the honour due to God alone. Pride puts self in the first place, greed puts money, lust puts pleasure, and gluttony makes a god of our food. For some it is power or ambition that holds pride of place in the heart – whatever we delight in, depend on and serve more than God constitutes our 'idol' (cf. 1 John 5:21). We are in trouble when this 'thing' pushes God off the throne of our hearts.

God also forbade the use of graven images (v.4); this was to make Israel unique among the nations who all represented their myriad gods in carved statues. The belief was that the image somehow gave you control over the god, but the Lord would not be manipulated by anyone! He showed Himself *without* form on Sinai (Deuteronomy 4:12) and wanted to be worshipped in faith. The incident of the Golden Calf (Exodus 32) will show how necessary was this prohibition, but modern archaeology shows that Israel remained faithful after that disastrous sin, which met with summary punishment. No carved images have been found in excavation of biblical sites, though quantities of such things have been unearthed in the surrounding countries.

This command was given because the Lord is a 'jealous' God, not jealous in our use of the term, but a God who demanded undivided loyalty from His people. Idolatry – which was an insult to His majesty and holiness – would never be tolerated. Instead it would be severely punished (v.5) (cf. Habakkuk 2:18), and there would be collective responsibility in the keeping or breaking of the Covenant, because God was dealing with the Israelites as a nation. Hence the sins of the fathers would be visited on the children to the third and fourth generation, but the generosity of God to those who kept the Covenant would far surpass this, going on to affect thousands (of generations. NAB).

The number one in scripture represents unity and primacy. Unity is indivisible and independent of all others – as is the Lord our God. 'Hear, O Israel, the Lord your God is one Lord' (Deuteronomy 6:4). It marks the beginning of number as God is the beginning of all things. This first commandment declares the primacy of God over all creatures. He is sovereign Lord, to be worshipped in spirit and in truth (John 4:24) – the Alpha and the Omega – the first and the last, the only love of our hearts and lives. If this commandment is obeyed, all the others fall into place.

The second commandment (20:7)[1]
The second command of God follows on from the first by demanding that God's name be held and used with reverence. The ancient world believed that its gods became present when their names were invoked, so they used these names in oaths, curses, magic and superstitious practices. God forbade all this. He was living among His people and would not tolerate the misuse of His Divine Presence. The taking of oaths was not forbidden to the people (Deuteronomy 10:20; Jeremiah 44:25; Matthew 23:16), but they developed such a reverence for the divine name that later in their history it was never pronounced. Other titles were used to denote the Lord's presence such as *Adonai* (Lord) or 'The Holy One of Israel' or 'The Power' or 'The Most High' (cf. Matthew 26:64). Jesus continued this great tradition when He taught us to pray 'Hallowed be Thy Name'. If we understand anything of who God is, then we will use His Name with reverence.

The third commandment (20:8–11)
'Remember the Sabbath day and keep it holy.' The Sabbath was a very ancient observance (Exodus 16:23) which was incorporated into the Decalogue in order to perpetuate it. It demanded that six days be given to work followed by a day of rest (Exodus 23:12, 34:21), in which God would be honoured as creator (v.11). No religious rites were ordered for it. As Jesus later stressed, this day was 'made for man' (Mark 2:27), for our benefit. At first it *was* simply a day of rest, but later in her history Israel's leaders imposed religious activities, and gradually so many

[1] Here I am following the Catholic-Lutheran division of the Commandments: c1 vv.2–6; c2 v.7; c3 vv.8–11; c4–8 vv.12–16, c9–10 v.17a,b. The Reformed Churches use the following division: c1 vv.2–3; c2 vv.4–6; c3 v.7; c4 vv.8–11; c5–10 vv.12–17. The Jews read v.2 as c1, vv.3–6 as c2, and the rest as the Reformed Churches.

rules grew up around it that the Sabbath was impossible to observe. Jesus spoke out against these abuses but did not lay aside the Sabbath rest. The early Christians observed this rest on a Sunday to commemorate the Resurrection of Jesus. Today, as the Jews observe Sabbath on Saturdays and the Christians on Sundays, we have a weekly commemoration of creation and redemption to keep our minds attuned to the wonderful works of God.

The fourth commandment (20:12)

The first three commands regulate our relationship with the Lord. The last seven deal with our relationships with each other. Together they deal with the vertical and horizontal aspects of faith and can be summed up in the two great laws which summarize the old and the new Law: 'You shall love the Lord your God with your whole heart and your whole soul, and your whole mind and your whole being, and you shall love your neighbour as yourself. This is the meaning of the whole Law and the Prophets' (Matthew 22:37–40). Jesus taught us that the way to show our love to God – apart from keeping His commandments – is to love and serve your neighbour (cf. John 13:34; 1 Corinthians 13; 1 John 4).

This commandment demands that we honour and reverence our nearest neighbours – those who gave us life. It is addressed primarily to adults, demanding that they give to ageing parents the care and love that they themselves received as children. Honouring the parents also demands that the offspring live in such a way as not to bring shame on parents in their old age. It includes filial respect, gratitude and love. It ensures that parents do not die in lonely isolation, unloved and uncared for. Severe penalties followed the violation of this command (cf. Exodus 21:17; Leviticus 20:9; Deuteronomy 21:18–21), and St Paul tells us that it was the only commandment which carried a promise, '. . . and you will have long life in the land' (v.12; Ephesians 6:2). Jesus fully obeyed this command when He subjected Himself to Mary and Joseph for thirty years in Nazareth, and also when he took care of His mother's needs before He died (Luke 2:52; John 19:26–27).

The fifth commandment (20:13)

'Thou shalt not kill.' This very complete statement aims at safeguarding the sacredness of human life from its beginning to its ending, declaring that God alone can give and take life. It forbade the deliberate killing of man by unauthorized persons. The penalty for such actions was death. Even the accidental killing of another person was considered very serious; the accused had to flee to cities of refuge to escape the avenger (cf. Deuteronomy 21:1–9). The command did not prohibit war. In conquering the Promised Land the people were commanded to exterminate whole cities and leave nothing alive (cf. Deuteronomy 20:10–20). Jesus raised this command to an altogether higher level when He declared anger to be the cause of murder and demanded that the anger be dealt with at source (Matthew 5:21–26; 1 John 3:15).

The sixth commandment (20:14)

The sanctity of marriage and the security of home life are protected by the sixth command. The breaking of this commandment, as with the fourth and fifth, also incurred the death penalty, in this case for both guilty partners (cf. Deuteronomy 22:22–27; John 8:1–11). It was considered to be great wickedness (Genesis 20:9, 33:9) for which even the great King David could not escape condemnation (cf. 2 Samuel 12:5–15). Jesus raised this command to a new level also by showing that the root cause of adultery is the lust hidden in the heart. He demanded that we should deal with this lust in order to keep our homes and our relationships in order (Matthew 5:27–30).

The seventh commandment (20:15)
This commandment was given to secure private ownership of property and promote honest dealings among the people. It seems that the theft of persons as well as material objects came under this law, which would prevent innocent people from being kidnapped and sold into slavery (Exodus 21:16; Deuteronomy 24:7).

The eighth commandment (20:16)
This commandment aims at protecting innocent people from false accusation, gossip and tale-bearing of all kinds, because of the damage caused to character and to relationships within the community. It also condemns the perjured testimony in the law courts. Jesus taught that this commandment meant that we must be committed to the truth in everything we do and say (Matthew 5:33–37).

The ninth and tenth commandments (20:17)
These two commandments condemn the interior state that leads a person to enter an illicit relationship with another man's wife or to appropriate his property. They point – as Jesus did later – to the root cause of trouble between neighbours, which is a wrong desire for the possessions of others (cf. James 4:1–2).

Putting the ten commandments together we see that God wanted to secure His own Lordship over the nation and then to protect each person's right to life, home, property and a society run on a basis of proper relationships. The number ten represents the perfection of divine order, a complete cycle with nothing missing, so these ten words of the Lord contain all that is necessary, no more and no less. Lived out, they would create a society at peace with God and man.

The book of the Covenant (20:22–23:19)

Exodus 24:7 gives this title to the various civil and judicial laws which form part of the Mosaic Law; the rest can be found in Leviticus (The Law of Holiness), Numbers and Deuteronomy. By the time these books were written, the people were in the process of change from a nomadic life in the wilderness to a settled life in Canaan. Their legal code developed over a period of time and resembles that of other Middle East countries at that time, like the Code of Hammurabi from the Babylonian Empire, although no evidence of actual borrowing is claimed. Unlike those other nations Israel adapted her laws to the Covenant relationship with the Lord so that the breaking of a law, civil or otherwise, was an offence against God (Deuteronomy 17:1, 22:5–12).

The book of the Covenant deals with civil and penal laws (21–22:14), laws concerning worship (20:22–26, 22:28–30, 23:10–18) and morality (22:16–27, 23:1–9). This whole section is completed by some preliminary instructions for the entry into the land of Canaan. The Lord promises the Israelites a guardian angel to accompany them on their journey (23:20–23). They must respect him and follow his guidance, for he is to stand in God's place. On entering the Promised Land the Lord will exterminate their enemies gradually (in fact they were never fully driven out). They were to make no peace pacts with their enemies, for that would prove to be a snare (vv.27–33). He named the boundaries of the Promised Land as the Sea of Reeds on the south, the Philistine Sea on the west (the Mediterranean), the Desert of Arabia on the east, and the River Euphrates on the north. Only in the era of David and Solomon was Israel to control this whole area (1 Kings 4:24, 5:1).

Israel called her Law 'The Torah', which means an instruction rather than a legal code. It was more a manifestation of God's will for His people to grow in holiness. The Torah is the most sacred part of the Bible for the Jews because it was given on Sinai with the Covenant. From the beginning the leaders urged the people to meditate on the Torah day and night, so that they could obey every word of it (John 1:8; Psalms 19,119). It was the source of life and grace for them, and became their rule of life and the source of all future reforms. Zeal for the Law was taken as a sign of holiness; some of the people even gave their lives for it (1 Maccabees 2:23–28).

By the time of Jesus many commentaries had been written on the Torah, and various schools of thought interpreted it differently. Oral tradition had developed also, and some teachers claimed that this too had Sinai as its source, and so was divinely inspired. The response to the Law was very narrow and legalistic. Jesus was to restore the spirit of the Law where the letter of the Law had taken over (Matthew 5:20; chapter 23). For His disciples, Jesus set aside the Law of Moses; they were to 'shoulder His yoke' instead, which is the law of love (John 13:34).

So Israel had her Covenant and Law. What she needed now was liturgy and worship. The Covenant stood on the basis of her obedience, but provision had to be made for failure or all was lost, because the people were sinful and would always be that way. The Covenant did not change this fact, so God in His mercy provided them with the altar of sacrifice (Exodus 20:24–28).

One of the functions of Law is to show up sin and transgression (Romans 7); this highlights our inability to keep God's Law by ourselves (Romans 7:8–10) and our desperate need for a saviour (Galatians 3:19, 23, 24). Each of the commandments touched upon areas of real sinfulness in man, which would be corrected by observing them (cf. Luke 18:18–23). God's wonderful provision for His people's weakness will be seen in the following chapters of Exodus, 25–40.

11. God Lives With Us

The Tabernacle (Exodus 25–31, 35–40)

'By your grace you led the people you redeemed,
By your strength you guided them to your *HOLY
 HOUSE.*'

(Exodus 15:13)

The Lord achieved His first goal in redemption when He led His people triumphantly out of Egypt. Now we come to His second goal, which was to lead them into His own dwelling place. The final goal was the occupation of the Promised Land, which is dealt with in the Book of Joshua.

The Lord said to Moses: 'Build me a sanctuary so that I may dwell among them' (25:8). The Book of Exodus devotes thirteen chapters to the erection of the first dwelling place of God on earth, describing both the building and the furnishings in minute detail. Not to ask 'Why?' would leave us bereft of much teaching that would illuminate our understanding of Church, priesthood and liturgy, for their foundations are here in the sanctuary of God in the wilderness, which was a heavenly model revealed by God to Moses (25:9; Hebrews 8:5). In it God revealed a whole system of worship which would both glorify His holiness and meet the needs of sinners at the same time, thus enabling the Covenant relationship to be sustained down through the centuries of man's infidelity to God's grace and calling (cf. 2 Timothy 3:16).

The episode of the golden calf (Exodus 32) showed up the need among the people for something external – like the Tabernacle and the Ark it contained – to act as a focus for worship in an idol-less religion. They had demanded an

185

external representation of the Lord, something they could see and touch, for they could not cope with His invisible presence. God's response to this need was – as always – marvellous. He gave them a portable Temple called the Tabernacle or Sanctuary or Tent of Meeting. Its structure was a pictorial illustration of the sanctuary of God in heaven (Hebrews 8:5) while at the same time foreshadowing Christ, who is the full manifestation of God in Himself (John 2:19; Hebrews 1:3) and spoke of the glory of Christ in His Church. As we shall see, Jesus is both priest, victim, mediator and sanctuary (John 15:1,5). As priest He serves the heavenly sanctuary before the throne of God (Hebrews 8:1–3). The earthly Tabernacle is a copy of this heavenly one, and through it God revealed many wonderful things (cf. Revlation 15:5; Ezekiel 1:26–28; Isaiah 6:1–5; Psalm 24).

Jesus is, in Himself, all that the sanctuary represented (Zechariah 6:12; John 2:19), for the fullness of the divinity (the Shekinah Glory) was in Him (Colossians 2:9) and He reconciled the world to God in Himself (2 Corinthians 5:19), completing the work of redemption in His own body (Hebrews 10:4–7). He came in the incarnation to place His Tabernacle – or pitch His tent – among us (John 1:14), thus making God personally and visibly present to mankind and fulfilling literally all that the Tabernacle represented: 'Here God lives among men. He will make his home among them; they shall be His people, and He will be their God; His name is God-with-them' (Revelation 21:3). The Church is now the visible presence of Jesus on earth, living His life and fulfilling His mission, gifted and guided by His Spirit and looking forward to the final fulfilment of the Tabernacle in the New Jerusalem (Revelation 21).

The Tabernacle was God's temporary dwelling place, to be used during the years of wandering in the wilderness. It was humble and lowly; the desert itself was the floor and the outer court was open to the sky. Nevertheless, it was the meeting place between God and man, and was a fitting pointer to the humble and lowly presence of God among

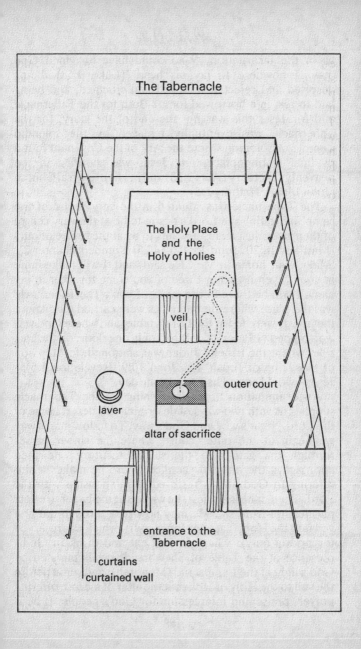

us in the incarnation. Who could have imagined *God* 'having nowhere to lay his head' (Luke 9:58), being despised and rejected, mocked and crucified, and being laid to rest in a borrowed tomb? Both for the Tabernacle and for Jesus this was not the end of the story, for the Tabernacle was eventually replaced by the splendid Temple of Solomon where the Ark of the Covenant found its final resting place, and Jesus was glorified in the heavenly sanctuary (Acts 2:33) and in His universal Church (John 14:6; 1 Timothy 2:5).

The Tabernacle was situated in the very centre of the camp, indicating the Lord's desire to be at the very centre of their lives, just as Jesus wants to be at the centre of ours (Matthew 18:20; John 15:4–6, 14:23; Numbers chapter 2). 'Make your home in Me,' He said, and 'I will make mine in you'; 'even if two or three of you come together in my name I will be there in the midst of you'. The Tabernacle was the place where the sacrifices were carried out, where the priests were fed at the Lord's table, and where God was worshipped (1 Peter 2:5). It had only one door, on the east side, where the tribe of Judah was stationed, for 'the lion of the Tribe of Judah' (cf. John 10:9; Revelation 5:5) – Jesus – would enter His Temple one day.

An examination of the furnishings of the Tabernacle supplies us with two ways of describing this desert home of the Lord – man's way and God's way. To follow man's way we begin at the outer court, where the sinner passes through the gate into the sacred territory. He then approaches the altar of sacrifice where he makes a sin-offering to God and is restored to relationship with the Lord. Then, if he is a priest, he washes at the Laver to effect purification from sin. He may now pass through the first veil into the Holy Place (or Inner court, which was reserved for priests only), where he can eat and drink in God's presence at the Table of Shewbread; be illuminated by God's light at the Lampstand (Menorah); and stand before the veil to the Holy of Holies at the altar of incense offering prayer, praise and intercession for God's people. If he is the High Priest he may now enter through the veil into the Holy of Holies (or Most Holy Place) and adore God at the Throne of Mercy over the Ark of the Covenant. These seven stages illustrate the progression of the sinner from repentance, through purification to enter into union with God (cf. Proverbs 4:18).

God's method of approaching the same reality is one of progressive revelation of Himself. He comes all the way from the Throne of Mercy to meet the sinner where he is, outside the gate. This is the order followed by the authors of Exodus showing God's desire to meet with us: The Ark (25:10–16), the Mercy Seat (25:17–22), the Table (25:23–30), the Lampstand (25:31–40), the Curtained Wall (26:1–14), the Framework (26:15–30), the Veil (26:31–37), the Altar of Sacrifice (27:1–8), the Outer Court (27:9). It is also the order followed by Jesus in the incarnation, where He left the glory of His Godhead behind (Philippians 2:6–10) and came among us to seek out the lost sheep and the sinners who could not make their way to Him (1 Peter 3:18; Luke 10:33, 15:4, 20:21).

St Paul seems to have had this double plan in mind – namely the sinner coming to God and God coming to the sinner – when he described in Romans the progression from sin through repentance to grace and glory (Romans 1–8) and, in Ephesians 1:4, our calling before the foundation of the world; this calling invites us to enter into our heavenly inheritance in Christ.

The most costly materials were used in the making of the Tabernacle so that its beauty would glorify God and be an uplift to the people (cf. Psalm 84:1–2, 4). The despoiling of the Egyptians had been necessary after all! (Exodus 12:36). Each item used carried special significance: the fabrics, for example, were purple – indicating royalty – blue (RSV) or violet (JB) indicating heavenly origin; red and crimson, denoting suffering; and white linen representing holiness. The metals were gold indicating divinity and royalty; silver representing redemption; and bronze denoting sin. Acacia wood, which was held to be incorruptible. represented the sacred humanity of Jesus, and the exquisite spices used for incense told of His pleasing intercession for us before God; the precious stones tell of His priestly perfection.

The Ark of the Covenant (25:10–16, 37:1–9)
This was a precious chest or box made of acacia wood which was overlaid with gold inside and out so that it appeared to be all gold. The Ark was the most important object in the tabernacle; without it the sanctuary would be meaningless, for the Lord used it as His throne (Isaiah 4:4). It was said to have been made by Moses himself, the only object in the Tabernacle made by him (Deuteronomy 10:1–5). The chest contained the two Tables of Stone on which the Ten Living Words were inscribed, a gold pot containing manna, and Aaron's rod (Hebrews 9:4); these latter objects were placed there at a later date. At the beginning and at the end of its history the ark contained only 'The Testimony' (25:16; 1 Kings 8:9) – the Tables of Stone stored under the Lord's Throne as a witness of the Covenant relationship.

The Ark was a type of Christ, its wood and gold pointing to His humanity and divinity. Its contents were the Word of God (ten commandments), the bread of God (manna), and Aaron's rod (priestly office). Jesus our High Priest is both the Word of God (John 1:1–2) and the Bread of Life for us (John 6) fulfilling, in Himself, the deepest needs of humanity. The Ark was the visible manifestation of the presence of God among His people; it gave them the security of knowing that He was with them (Exodus 25:8; 1 Samuel chapters 4–6; 1 Kings 8:1–13, etc.) It did not *contain* God's presence, but the Shekinah Glory rested on it (Numbers 7, 8, 9). So, too, with Jesus, in whom the Shekinah Glory was seen fully: 'to have seen Me is to have seen the Father' (cf. John 10:29, 12:45, 14:9). When the Son of God became incarnate in the womb of the Virgin Mary she, too, became a fulfilment of the Ark of the Covenant. This means that she was the precious container

190

of Him who is both Word and Bread and Priest. She was a more glorious manifestation of God than the Ark, for she contained within her womb the Shekinah Glory of God, He who *is* the Mercy Seat of God – hence the Church calls her 'Mother of Mercy'.

The Mercy Seat or Propitiatory was the solid gold lid of the Ark; on it two golden cherubs were depicted in an attitude of adoration, with their wings covering the whole slab. The Shekinah Glory manifested itself between the two cherubim (25:17–22; 2 Chronicles 3:10–12). The Hebrew word used for the Mercy Seat is *Kapporeth*, which means both a 'lid' and a 'cover' and also 'to perform an expiation'. Thus it was the place of God's justice where sin had to be expiated on the Day of Atonement (*Yom Kippur*) by the sprinkling of sacrificial blood (Leviticus 16:14); but it was also the Mercy of God shown to sinners (cf. Romans 3:25; 1 John 2:2, 4:10; Hebrews 9:5; Revelation 5:6) for God wanted His Throne to be a place of communion not of judgement (cf. Numbers 7, 8, 9). Jesus has fulfilled the sprinkling of the Mercy Seat for ever (Hebrews 9:11–14) and gives us daily cleansing from sin (1 John 2:1–2) so that we can remain in union with God. Because of this we can come boldly and confidently, before the Throne of Grace where we find mercy and grace awaiting us, not judgement (Hebrews 4:14; Romans 8:1).

The Table of Shewbread (25:23–30, 37:10–16)
The Holy Place – which was used only by priests – had three pieces of furniture: the Table, the Lampstand (or *Menorah*) and the Altar of Incense. The Table, like the Ark, was made of acacia wood overlaid with gold. Twelve loaves of bread were laid upon it and remained in God's presence for seven days before being eaten by the priests. Because of this it was called the 'bread of the Presence' (NAB, RSV, NIV) or the 'bread of continual offering' (JB) (v.30; Numbers 4:7). The loaves represented the twelve tribes in Covenant with the Lord. The table was the

The Holy Place and the Holy of Holies

Holy Place

Ark of the Covenant

Holy of Holies

veil

Altar of Incense

Table of Shewbread

Menorah (lampstand)

veil

The Ark

Communion Table where the representatives of the people – the priests – could eat and drink in God's presence, for the libation was associated with the Communion (37:16; Leviticus 24:5–9). The table points to God's desire to have fellowship and communion with us; it found its fulfilment in the eucharistic table of Jesus, our Lord, who lives continually in God's presence and in the sacrament of the Eucharist as the spiritual food for this priestly people (John 6; 1 Peter 2:9). To partake of this table implies identification with Christ as well as communion with Him (1 Corinthians 10:14–22).

The Lampstand (Menorah) (25:31–40, 37:17–24)

Since the Holy Place was a closed structure, cut off from the sunlight, it needed the lampstand to provide light. It was a seven-branched lampstand, and made of solid gold, which looked like a flowering almond tree and was called the watchful or vigilant tree (cf. Jeremiah 1:11, 12), for the vigil light perpetually burned in God's presence (27:20). It pointed to the fact that God alone (the gold) is light and the illuminator of all men (John 1:9), and He keeps watch over all His creation (Zechariah 4:1–14, especially 10b). Its lamps were fed with oil (27:20–21; Leviticus 24:1–4).

The sevenfold radiance of the *Menorah* not only reflects the perfection of light (God), but points to Jesus as the perfect manifestation of God *as* light (John 8:12). It also foreshadows the sevenfold manifestation of the Holy Spirit upon the Church (Isaiah 11:1–6), which enables believers to 'walk in the light' (John 8:12) by illuminating the inner depths of the teaching of Jesus (John 14:26) and bringing them to recognize Jesus as the bread of life – since the Table and the Lampstand stood together in the Holy Place. It also lit up the Altar of Incense, pointing to the Holy Spirit's role in forming communities of prayer, praise and intercession before God for the world, thus making *them* into lampstands! (cf. Matthew 5:14; Revelation 1:20).

Christians have access to the Holy Spirit because the

death and Resurrection of Jesus rent the veil (Matthew 27:51) and opened the way for us to go into God's presence (Hebrews 9:19–25) and commune with Him. Because we have personally entered into His Redemptive process we are free to enjoy His light, commune at His table, and offer our worship of prayer and praise at His throne. Those outside of redemption, who do not have this privilege, are 'in darkness'.

There will be no natural light in the New Jerusalem, where the Church will achieve her goal as the Bride of the Lamb (Jesus). She will be illuminated 'by the radiant glory of God' (Revelation 21:23). The Lamb Himself will then be her lampstand (Revelation 2:6) just as He is during the present age of the Church (Hebrews 1:3). The *Menorah* stands for the fact that Jesus is the light of the Old Law, the New Law, and Heaven, and His enlightening work is done through the Holy Spirit.

The Altar of Incense (30:1–10; 37:25–29)
This last piece of furniture in the Holy Place was 'an altar of supreme holiness' (v.10). It was called the Golden Altar because it was made of acacia wood overlaid with gold (v.1–4, 39:38) and it was placed in front of the veil separating the High Priest from the Holy of Holies directly opposite the Ark (v.6.).

This altar represents Christ (acacia wood and gold) in His ministry of intercession as high priest before the throne of God in the heavenly sanctuary, where He makes the fruits of His sacrifice continually available to us (John 17; Hebrews 7:25, 13:10–16; Romans 8:33–34).

Incense was used in all pagan worship in ancient times. For God's people it was to·become a symbol of prayer rising up before His throne, its fragrance pleasing to Him so that He would accept the intercessions of the people through their priest-mediator (Psalm 141:2; Revelation 5:8). It was composed of very costly spices blended into a beautiful perfume. Only consecrated priests could burn this pure and holy incense before God (30:34–37). Any sinner who presumed to take this privilege upon himself met with summary punishment (2 Chronicles 26:16–21).

Curtains and hangings (26:1–14, 36:8–19)
These formed the internal protective coverings for the Tabernacle, shutting off sunlight, for the Shekinah Glory was to be the only light of the Holy of Holies. They were made of white linen with purple fabric; violet (blue), red and crimson had been used to embroider cherubim upon them. Over the curtains a tent was hung made of rams' skins dyed red with badgers' skins on the outside. There were ten white linen curtains, and the priests had to be clothed in white linen when ministering in the Tabernacle (28:39–43; Leviticus 16:4).

The ten white linen curtains represent the spotless holiness of Christ, and the Church's holiness is also depicted as the Bride of the Lamb dressed in dazzling white linen (Revelation 19:8–9). The message is that without holiness no one can enter into God's presence (Hebrews 12:14). The other colours used tell us that our heavenly (blue) King (purple) is also our redeemer (red) who suffered for us (crimson). Whenever the priests served in the sanctuary they beheld those colourful cherubs embroidered on the white linen; this allowed them to behold a pictorial representation of the coming redeemer. It is interesting to note that cherubs guarded not only the Ark but the Tabernacle itself – their duty being to protect God's holiness and prevent anything unworthy from coming into His presence (cf. Genesis 3:24). The heavenly sanctuary (of which this is only a model) also has these wonderful spirits around God's throne in praise and worship, ready to execute His judgements on the earth (Revelation 5:11–14). The psalmist, however, did not find them threatening figures, but a sign of protection; he wanted to take refuge in the shelter of those wings (Psalms 17:8, 61:4, 91:4).

These glorious inner walls were seen only by those who were permitted entrance beyond the veil – in those days, priests. They point to the fact that only those who enter into deep communion with God in prayer can taste the true glories of the mysteries of Christ, which are hidden from 'the world' or 'those outside'. The world beholds something very different – just a tent of animal skins. This points to His rejection by an unbelieving world that does not grasp the mystery of Him who made Himself of no reputation for us. Because of this He has no beauty to attract the eyes (Isaiah 53) – that is reserved for those who enter within and behold His glory (John 2:12; 1 John 1:1–4).

The framework of the Tabernacle was made from bars of acacia wood plated with gold; these stood in silver sockets signifying that our redeemer brings sinners into intimacy with God on the ground of redemption (silver) (24:15–30, 36:20–34).

The Veil and the Door (26:31–37, 36:35–38)

The precious cloth of the veil hung between the Holy Place and the Holy of Holies cutting off the Ark of the Covenant from the view of the priests; it too was made of fine white linen with cherubim embroidered on it in purple, red and blue. It too pointed to Christ, who *is* the veil, or means of access to God, for us; it depicted His holiness, His heavenly origin, His cross and His crown. The cherubim here protect the Throne of the Lord from the access of sinners, just as they protected the Tree of Life in Paradise (Genesis 3:24).

Before the incarnation of Christ there was no access to God beyond the veil, except for the High Priest on the Day of Atonement. Yet even here Jewish tradition tells us that they tied a rope around his ankle in the event of his entering the Holy of Holies with his sins unforgiven, for he would thus incur instant death (Leviticus 16:2; Isaiah 6:1–6; Hebrews 9:25). Since no one else could go beyond the veil, they could then pull his dead body out with the rope. The veil kept the people of Israel at a distance from God for the full duration of the Sinaitic Covenant (Exodus 19:12–13, 18–20), but with the death of Jesus everything has changed. Now through Him 'we *have* the right to enter the sanctuary by a new way which he has opened for us, *a living opening through the curtain (veil)*, that is to say his body' (Hebrews 10:19–20). When the High Priest went beyond the veil he could not go empty-handed; he had to take sacrificial blood and sweet smelling incense with him. In His sacrificial death Jesus made full expiation for sin at the throne of God (Matthew 27:51; Hebrews 4:14, 6:19, 9:12; Leviticus 4:6). At the moment of His death the veil in the Temple was torn down the middle (Luke 23:45), thus exposing the Throne of Grace and Mercy, and giving confidence to all sinners to come close to God (Hebrews 10:22).

The door at the entrance of the Tabernacle was a screen made of the same material as the other hangings. Unlike the veil it gave admittance into God's presence, and points to Christ as the 'door' or 'gate' through whom we gain admittance into the House of God (John 10:9; Exodus 26:36–37).

The Altar of Sacrifice (27:1–8, 38:1–7)
Walking through the door from the Holy Place into the Outer Court we come to the bronze altar, so called because it was made of acacia wood plated with bronze. The 'horns of the altar' were four projections at its corners and were considered especially sacred. A guilty person who clung to the horns of the altar was looked upon as clinging to God for protection and so escaped punishment (1 Kings 1:50, 2:28–29). This altar was the centre of the whole sacrificial system and prepared the people for an understanding of the mystery of Christ's death on Calvary. Without this preparation redemption by sacrifice would have been incomprehensible.

The sinner who entered the sanctuary had to bring an

animal with him as a substitute for himself: an innocent animal must die in place of the guilty person. Without this sacrifice there was no access to God, for blood sacrifice was the ground of approach to Him. The acacia wood speaks of the humanity of Christ, and the bronze of judgement (Numbers 21:9; Deuteronomy 28:23; Judges 16:21; Revelation 1:15, etc.). So the altar represented Jesus as the victim for sin who would give His life for us – hence it was the altar which sanctified the gift upon it (29:37; Matthew 23:19). It continually reminds us that the cross of Christ is the source of our blessing and grace and our privileged access to God.

The outer court (27:9–19)
The outer 'wall' of the Tabernacle was made of white linen hangings supported on sixty pillars. These indicated the holiness of Him who dwelt within, in marked contrast to the unholiness of the people who 'tented' or 'tabernacled' all around Him. A holy God in the midst of an unholy people! The 'walls' spoke too of the principle of inclusion and exclusion; within was the sacred space where all that pertained to God was executed, while outside all that was secular was carried out. The sinners outside were separated from the Throne of the Lord – the Throne of Mercy and Grace – by three 'gates'. First, the door to the outer court illustrated the great distance between the sinner and God, but this was shortened by the sacrifices on the bronze altar. Once sprinkled with the blood of the victim, the priest-sinner could then go through the second 'gate' into the Holy Place, but even he was permanently separated from entering the Holy of Holies by the third 'gate' – the veil.

The whole description of the Tabernacle with its outer court of sixty pillars is very similar to a passage in the Song of Songs (3:6–11), where the curtained litter of King Solomon is described as coming up from the desert carried by sixty warriors. It too was made of wood, silver and gold, coloured purple, and smelled of sweet incense. Here, the Tabernacle, the temporary home of the Lord, the King of

Israel, is carried through the wilderness on its sixty pillars, showing that God their king lived with them. They, therefore, entered the courts of this great king – the Lord – with praise and thanksgiving, realizing how privileged they were among the nations of the earth (cf. Psalms 65:4, 84:2, 92:13, 100:4; Isaiah 1:12).

The laver or bronze basin (30:17–21)

This seventh and last piece of furniture in the Tabernacle was for the purification of priests only. It pointed to the need for continuous purification among those who would seek intimacy with God, for nothing defiled or unclean can enter His presence (Revelation 21:27). The priests washed their hands and feet with water, showing that our work (hands) and 'ways' or lifestyle (feet) need constant renewal, the renewal obtained from applying daily the Word of God (water) to our lives (cf. Ephesians 5:25 (RSV, NAB); John 15:3; Psalm 119:9). Jesus spoke of something very similar to the laver when he addressed his first priests – the Apostles – telling them that their baptism (the 'bath') gave them entrance into the Kingdom of God. What they needed now was cleansing, represented in the washing of the feet (John 13:8–11; see Exodus 29:4).

The priesthood (chapters 28, 29, 39)

The Tabernacle could not function without an official priesthood, chosen by God for this special task (Hebrews 5:4) and publicly consecrated to Him and His service (28:1). The priests were to act as mediators between the Lord and Israel, and would enjoy greater privileges and intimacy with Him. This, too, was according to the pattern given by God on the mountain (25:40) and foreshadowed things to come (Hebrews 8). Aaron, his sons and their descendants (Levites) were chosen and consecrated by Moses for their office (chapter 29). God ordained that they should wear vestments when carrying out their duties (chapter 28) – both to express the dignity and glory of their vocation (28:2) and their priestly role on behalf of the people. All this has deep significance for us, for when the priest stood robed before the people he foreshadowed the glory of Christ to come, but standing before the Lord he symbolized all the steps needed to gain access to God.

The tribe of Levi were not chosen for any holiness in them. No! Aaron had taken a leading role in the idolatrous worship of the golden calf. They were sinner-priests, chosen by sovereign grace to represent their sinner-nation before God. It was God's choice which raised them very high (the meaning of Aaron's name) both in the sight of God and of the people. Aaron was called to foreshadow the *pattern* of Jesus' priesthood (Acts 5:31; Hebrews 4:14), although it was of a much lower order. Jesus' priesthood was of the order of Melchizedek (Hebrews 7). The Aaronic priesthood ended during the Passion of Jesus when the high priest rent his garments – an action expressly forbidden by the Law (Matthew 26:65; Leviticus 21:10). This, coupled with the rending of the veil in the Temple (Matthew 27:51), signalled the ending of the Sinaitic Covenant, its priesthood and its sacrificial system.

The priestly garments (28:1–43)

Aaron was clothed in six garments that expressed his high priestly office: the breastplate (28:15–30), the ephod (28:6–14), the robe (28:31–35), the tunic (28:39), the mitre (28:36–38) and a girdle (28:8).

The ephod was like a white linen apron, with gold, purple, blue (violet), red and crimson embroidery on it. Two onyx stones were placed on the shoulder straps, each having the names of six of the Tribes engraved on them. This outer garment was considered especially sacred. Here we see the spotless holiness of Christ (white linen), our divine (gold and blue) king (purple) and redeemer (red and crimson). Wearing this ephod Aaron foreshadowed the true High Priest who was to carry God's people before the throne of grace for ever (onyx stones on the shoulders). As he stood there, the girdle around his waist (28:8) spoke of his readiness for service, just as Jesus would come to serve, and not to be served (Luke 12:37, 22:27; John 13:4–5, 14; Ephesians 6:14).

The breastplate, the most costly of the priest's garments, spoke of the very heart of Christ Himself. It was a square cloth made of fine white linen, attached to the ephod with blue lace and gold rings. It was worked with the same colours as the ephod. Twelve different precious stones were set in it in three rows of four, to show that God's people are precious in His eyes (cf. Isaiah 43:4), but distinct and separate and treated individually – called by name (Isaiah 43:1–2). The high priest was to carry them always in his heart, interceding for them before God (28:29). Jesus, our High Priest, carries His people in his heart (John 13:1), each one separate, known and yet loved – (John 13:23), tied to Him for ever with cords of love (cf. Isaiah 49:16; Hosea 11:4; Exodus 28:22–24).

The breastplate was also called the 'pectoral of judgement', because it contained the mysterious Urim and Thumim which were used by the high priest to discern God's will for the people (Numbers 27:21). The form the Urim and Thumin took is unknown. They are thought to have been precious stones which would light up in God's presence indicating a 'yes' or 'no' answer to the question given (28:30; cf. Proverbs 16:33; 1 Samuel 14:41–42, 23:10–12) when lots were drawn after prayer; it was accepted that God was thus indicating His will (cf. Acts 1:15–26).

The robe (28:31–35) made entirely of blue (violet) and purple was worn under the ephod and appears to have been seamless, with no sleeves. John's gospel (19:23) shows Jesus wearing the seamless robe as He went to His great sacrifice on Calvary. The robe was an emblem of royal dignity also (1 Samuel 24:4; 1 Chronicles 15:27; Ezekiel 26:16). Its hem was decorated with pomegranates and bells which would tinkle as Aaron entered and left the sanctuary. It is thought the function of the bells was to ward off the evil spirits who would be active around the sanctuary. The Evil One is ever anxious to thwart those who sincerely seek God.

The mitre for Aaron's head bore a gold plate with the awesome words 'sacred to the Lord' engraved on it, obviously a declaration of the sacredness of the priesthood and a constant reminder of the holiness demanded by it. The priest was to be 'holy' – that is, separate for the Lord, belonging to Him only, so much so that he had to bear the guilt of the people during their worship. He was responsible for their worship (28:38). How well this points to Christ, 'who bore our iniquities and carried our sins' (Isaiah 53:46), who is responsible for all our worship, which we carry out through Him, with Him and in Him.

The inner garments of the priests, worn next to the body, were a white linen tunic and breeches (28:39, 42), for they had to be clothed in purity and holiness (Psalm 132:9).

Consecration of priests (29:1–46, 30:22–33; Leviticus 8)
'You will then anoint and invest and consecrate them to serve me in the priesthood' (28:41). The priests were chosen from among their own brethren (28:1), and brought to the door of the Tabernacle (29:4) where they were fully bathed (29:4) before being clothed in their priestly vestments (29:4–9) and anointed with chrism (29:7,21). They proceeded to the altar of sacrifice, where three burnt offerings were made on their behalf. First the sin offering: a bull was brought; each one laid hands on it to signify the passing of guilt on to the victim, which was then immolated for them. Some of its blood was put on the horns of the altar, which signified their clinging to God for mercy; the rest was poured on the ground at its foot. Some of the entrails were burnt on the altar, but the bulk were burnt outside the camp, for sin was a leprosy of the soul in God's sight. This was followed by the offering of two rams to God, one as an appeasement or peace offering (29:15–18), and the second as the 'ram of consecration'. Here too the

priests laid hands on the ram to signify the handing over of their lives to God (29:23). The blood of the consecrated victim was touched to the right ear, right thumb and right big toe of the priest, and was sprinkled on his vestments with chrism (30:22–33) to consecrate them to the Lord's use only (29:19–21).

The anointing of the ear signified the opening of the ear to hear God's Word, because one of the priestly functions was to be God's oracle, discerning God's will and giving God's prophetic Word to Israel (cf. Deuteronomy 33:8–10). They were to be the special teachers of the Torah, guiding the people in its morality. On top of the function of teacher, guide and prophet, the special priestly role was offering sacrifice, although kings and prophets were permitted this privilege at a later date (cf. 1 Samuel 13:9–10; 2 Samuel 6:13–18; Judges 6:25–26, etc.). The specifically priestly act was the sprinkling or pouring of the blood of the victim on the altar. The animal could be killed by someone else (Exodus 24:3–8; Leviticus 1:5, 3:2, 8:13, etc.). The anointing of the hands and feet indicated the holiness demanded of priests in their works and their ways.

Following the sacrifice, the rite of 'filling their hands' was carried out (29:24–25) where one of the loaves of Shewbread was placed in Aaron's hands for him to offer to God. It was then burnt on the altar (*given* to God). From now on the priests would be cared for by the sanctuary; the people were obliged to support them financially (29:26–28, 30:11–16, cf. 1 Samuel 2;13; Leviticus 10:12–20; 1 Timothy 5:18). The ceremony was concluded by participation in the sacred meal (communion) which no lay person could share (29:31–35).

The consecration of the altar followed (29:36–37). This took seven days, for it was considered especially sacred (v.37). From then on a daily *holocaust* (burnt offering) of two lambs was offered morning and evening to keep the nation in right relationship with God (vv.38–40). With them a libation of oil and wine was offered; these were poured out on the ground after the offering so that they were irretrievable (v.41). This was the most sacred form of offering, because both the lambs and the libation were given over fully to God to represent what should have been the people's full surrender to God's will for them.

It was now accomplished! The Lord had brought the people to Himself in a place consecrated to His glory (v.43), with a consecrated priesthood and a liturgy worthy of Him. Now He could *really* be their God (v.45), they would now know who it was who brought them out of Egypt (v.46). Here we see the cry of God our saviour – the same cry, whether we find it in the Old or New Testament: 'Father, that they may *know* you, the only true God, and Jesus Christ whom you have sent . . . Consecrate them in the truth . . . keep them true to your name . . . (John 17). His desire is to manifest Himself to us (John 14:21) to make His home with us (John 14:23) . . . you in me and I in you . . . perfectly one' (John 17).

The atonement money (30:11–15)

The Lord, as ruler of Israel, now took the first census of the people (cf. Numbers, chapter 1). Each man of twenty years and over was obliged to pay a half shekel (about forty pence) as atonement money to the Tabernacle. It was later known as Temple Tax (cf. Matthew 17:26; 1 Peter 1:18–19). A census for military or tax purposes was a custom of kings in the ancient world, but Israel feared it as an encroachment on God's rights. Only He should know how many people He claimed as His own (cf. 1 Chronicles 21:1–4, 7, 8). The payment of the half shekel took the place of a census and provided revenue for the Tabernacle at the same time. It gave the Covenant personal meaning too, for in this way each man acknowledged his redemption by the Lord. The ransom was such that everyone could pay it. The rich were not allowed to give more or the poor less, for God would treat all His people equally, both in privileges and responsibilities.

God's workmen (31:1–11, 35:30–35)

God not only revealed the pattern of the Tabernacle to Moses, but also whom He had chosen to execute the task for Him. Bezalel from the tribe of Judah, and Oholiab from the tribe of Dan, were appointed, for God had filled them with the spirit of wisdom, understanding and knowledge (vv.1–6) (Oholiab was also given the gift of teaching so that he would oversee the engraving, weaving and craftwork) (35:34-35). The gifts given by the Holy Spirit were task-orientated – in other words each of those chosen was anointed for his mission, just as Moses had been for his – and their joint mission was to build God's house. The early Church also chose men for special tasks of building up the Church, after it had been discerned that they were gifted by the Holy Spirit for particular missions (Acts 6:1–6).

These men foreshadow Jesus, the Anointed One, who was given the Spirit without reserve (Isaiah 11:1–3; John 3:34), the one who came to build the Church, God's home on earth (Matthew 16:18). He, Himself *was* the Temple (John 2:19), incorporating us into it as living stones (1 Peter 2:5) for we are of His workmanship (Ephesians 2:10). The workmen were required to build the Tabernacle in exact obedience to God's plan (31:6, 36:1), just as Jesus did (John 6:38, 14:31).

Before the actual building commenced we are again reminded of the sacredness of the Sabbath rest (vv.12–17) which was to be observed even during the building of the Tabernacle. No excuse, therefore, religious or secular, was accepted by God for breaking the Sabbath rest. This is a solemn charge, and we Christians need to take heed lest we find ourselves too busy on Sundays, doing religious things for God, instead of obeying His will and His clear command to REST!

The building completed (chapters 35–40)

These chapters repeat chapters 25–31, where the plan of the Tabernacle is given. Here we see the orders carried out. All the materials were free-will offerings (35:21), and anyone who could help was employed (35:26, 36:2). So the building of the Tabernacle was a labour of love by the people, they were so generous in their giving that Moses had to put a stop to the collection of materials! (36:5–7). Their generosity expressed their gratitude to the Lord for all His goodness to them. This is the spirit in which all collections and service are given to the Church so that it can be built up in love. God's commands were obeyed to the letter (36:8–40:33), and the Tabernacle was completed in the second year of the exodus from Egypt. From this we see that the people spent eighteen months at Sinai (40:17). Moses consecrated the Tabernacle, its furnishings and its priests so that all was ready for the Lord to 'come home'. The Cloud of God's presence came and filled the Tabernacle, and the Shekinah Glory was manifested so powerfully that even Moses could not enter the sanctuary! (40:34, 35). God was with them at last. He had made His home with them. He was no longer the devouring fire of Sinai, but the Glory of merciful love and grace reached out to sinners. Now he was 'our God' and 'our Lord' and they could journey on.

The Tabernacle today

We have see that the redemptive work of Christ was foreshadowed and prepared in Moses and the exodus. The Tabernacle prefigured our churches also, which are built on its model. Here, we too have our sanctuary, with its altar and sacred liturgy; we have our precious box containing the Shekinah Glory of God in the sacramental presence of Jesus, with its perpetual light shining outside declaring the Lord's presence within. We do not call this box an 'ark' but a 'tabernacle' – the most sacred part of the church. We, too, have our consecrated priests who exercise the priestly office of Jesus on our behalf, dressed in their sacred vestments. We have our daily Eucharist where the Church, perpetually, morning and evening, offers the Lamb of God sacramentally to the Father on our behalf, making effectual for us here and now all that Jesus wrought on Calvary. In it we retain the 'lavabo' or ritual washing of the priest's hands, the offering of bread and wine, the reading of the Word, the use of incense and intercessory prayers. As it is, our full public worship is performed by the whole mystical body of Jesus Christ, head and members, for we are His priestly people. From this we see that every liturgical celebration, because it is an action of Christ, the priest, and His body, the Church, is a sacred action beyond all others, and a foretaste of the heavenly liturgy in the New Jerusalem where Jesus sits at the right hand of God, the priest of the true tabernacle (cf. Revelation 21:2; Colossians 3:1; Hebrews 8:2). We join our praise with the heavenly choirs and venerate the memory of the saints who have reached this destination before us, and with whom we hope to have fellowship one day, and we declare our hope in our eager longing for Jesus' return on the clouds of heaven when we can join Him in glory (Revelation 5:6–14; Philippians 3:20; Colossians 3:4; cf. Vatican II, Sacred Liturgy Nos. 7, 80).

V. The Final Stage

12. Toward the Promised Land

The Golden Calf (Exodus 32:1–6)
We have seen the Covenant and the Tabernacle; we can now return to the story of Israel's pilgrimage. The full horror of her sin, which reveals the innate depravity of humanity, is best seen against the background of sovereign grace as displayed at Sinai.

The events narrated here are the historical sequel to chapter 19, where we saw Moses spend forty days on the mountain: here we see what transpired among the people in his absence. Forty days was a long time in a trackless wasteland; panic broke out and the people reverted to paganism (vv.1–2). The frightening aspect of it was that it occurred so soon after the glorious manifestation of God on Sinai, where he had proclaimed His almighty power and holiness, and the need of the people to purify themselves and keep a reverential distance (19:9–15); so soon after they had vowed in solemn covenant to keep His Law, of which the first commandment stated that they should not have any other gods or make graven images!

Here, while still encamped at Sinai, they formally broke the Covenant seal – apparently giving no thought to the consequences. They had left Egypt, but Egypt was still in their hearts (cf. Acts 7:39–43); the Lord was rejected in favour of the old ways of idolatry (cf. Joshua 24:14). Moses too, their divinely appointed deliverer, was referred to contemptuously as 'this man who brought us from Egypt' (32:1). Their action shows that many people in the nation just went along with the exodus, without any real conversion of heart. Such is the mystery of humanity in every age, for Christians, who just go along with the Church without experiencing conversion of heart, will also find that they have no security against a reversion to idol worship (cf. Deuteronomy 32:12; 1 Corinthians 10:6–8; 1 John 5:21; Revelation 2:4–6). Moses' absence was the trial which exposed Israel's heart, and Jesus' 'absence' during the age of the Church is what shows up ours. Jesus said, 'When I return shall I find *any* faith on earth?' (cf. Luke 18:8; Matthew 24:45–51, 25:1–46). Israel, like ourselves, had given lip service, but the Lord wanted the surrender of the heart (19:8, 20:19–20; Mark 7:6–7).

The people turned to Aaron, the priest, and demanded that he make for them 'a god to go ahead of them', for they had no idea what had become of Moses (32:1). Accordingly Aaron took their gold rings, melted them, cast them in a mould and 'out came the calf'! (vv.2, 3, 23–24). The effigy was brought before the people with the words: 'Here is your God, Israel – who brought you up from the land of Egypt' (v.4). Aaron then built an altar for the golden calf, declaring the following day as a festival 'in honour of the Lord'! At dawn the following day the feast began; offering holocausts and communion sacrifices were followed by eating and drinking. Then the people rose up to amuse themselves (v.6).

The so-called calf was most probably a bull representing the Egyptian god Apis or the Canaanite god Baal. It seems incredible that the Israelites would declare they had been delivered from Egypt by an *Egyptian* god! Archaeological evidence suggests that the bull was the throne of the Lord, who would sit on it. To control the bull this way was to show strength and power, and it was as such the Canaanites used it. Therefore the bull was not an image of God, but His glory was thus associated, not with the heavenly cherubim – as in the Tabernacle – but dragged down to the level of the beasts of the field and the nature gods of the pagans (cf. Ezekiel 20:8; 1 Kings 12:26–33; 2 Kings 10:29: de Vaux p. 334). The Psalmist's comment was that they had exchanged the one who was their glory (the Lord) for the image of a grass-eating ox! (Psalm 106:20). Here we see how ludicrous this sin – and all sin – is. Not only had the Israelites forfeited the Shekinah Glory, but with it they fell from its lofty standards of purity and morality to indulge in pagan orgies, which showed that they too had fallen to the level of the beasts of the field, for we become like that which we worship. The people wanted God's promises of relationship, protection, guidance and the Promised Land – but they were not prepared to pay the price of that privileged relationship, which was enshrined in: 'If you love me keep my commandments'! They had not the patience to wait on God's timing in setting up the Tabernacle. God and Moses delayed too long, so they went ahead anyway and set up their own external image (idol) with disastrous consequences. It was the 'flesh' in action, for we are here dealing with Romans 7 of the Book of the Exodus! (cf. Romans 7:14–25). How different everything would have been if they had waited patiently on the Lord! (Isaiah 40:31).

This episode gives us a powerful lesson in leadership, for Aaron was unable to govern the people as did his brother Moses, and allowed them to pressurize him into doing what was expressly forbidden. His actions, though inexcusable, would also be inexplicable unless we take cognisance of the Jewish tradition which states that Hur, who was co-ruler with Aaron (24:14), resisted the idolatry and was stoned to death (he is not mentioned again after this), thus frightening Aaron into compliance. Anarchy reigns in the absence of good leadership, and disaster follows when the true worship of God is mixed with schemes of the flesh: God seeks those who will worship Him in spirit and in truth (John 4:23), worthily, according to His ways.

Moses the Mediator (32:7–14)

Moses, deep in communion with God on the Mount, was informed of the corruption in the camp. In the revelation he received here of the Covenant and the Tabernacle, God had carved out a new way of life and worship for Israel, but she did not wait for it to be shown her (v.8). Jesus has shown us the way to the Father, but how many of us follow it? (John 14:6, 6:67–71). They had rejected God, and now God will not acknowledge them as *His* people (v.7). 'If you deny me before men I will disown you before my father', Jesus said (Matthew 10:33). The Covenant for them and for us is a two-way relationship: if we break it we release God from His Covenant-ownership of us, but the realization of this should keep us from sinning!

God saw not only the external act of idolatry but also the motive behind it. The problem was self-will, a refusal to surrender to God and His ways: it was to be 'stiffnecked' or 'headstrong' and this quality underlies all rebellion (cf. Isaiah 48:4; Zechariah 7:11; 2 Chronicles 30:8; Acts 7:51). Unfortunately union with God is not possible without the crucifixion of self-will and the surrender of the heart to Him. Because of this God said to Moses, 'Leave me now, my wrath will blaze out against them and devour them; of *you*, however, I will make a great nation' (v.10). Here God shows Moses that only *his* intercession can save the people now. If Moses goes away God's justice will work, but if he intercedes mercy will prevail. How necessary is the Redeemer!

Moses, as expected, rose to the occasion and interceded or 'stood in the breach' between God and Israel. The Lord was *his* God because Moses was not party to the rebellion (v.11). There was one good man left, and we shall see that the prayer of faith of a good man achieves much with God (Psalm 14:2; James 5:15). God had rejected the people, telling Moses that they were his (v.7), but Moses gently gave them back to God, declaring that the Lord was the Redeemer, not himself (v.11). He was only the go-between, God's representative to them, and their mediator with Him. He also brushed aside the temptation to become the head of a great nation if God were to begin again (v.10b), because Israel would *become* a great nation if only the relationship with God could be sorted out! The people had been idol-worshippers in Egypt and God knew this, yet He had worked great wonders on their behalf in order to release them from the house of bondage. Their conversion to Him would be slow, so God would have to show as much mercy now, as He did goodness before. He also pleaded that God's glory was at stake, for if the Lord wiped out Israel, Egypt could vent her hatred of the Lord and of Israel by declaring to the world that the Lord was weak and could not – or fickle and would not – save His people in the end (v.12; cf. Numbers 14:13–19; Joshua 7:9; Deuteronomy 9:28; Isaiah 48:9–11; Psalm 23:3). The Lord would have to forgive them for the sake of His own name, and for glory and righteousness. Finally Moses played his trump card when he pleaded God's *eternal* Covenant with Abraham: he appealed to God's faithfulness, and his intercession prevailed (vv.13–14).

Moses' intercession here foreshadows that of Jesus in John 17, where Jesus also declared that the people given to Him belonged to the Father (17:6) and that He would be glorified in them, becoming the new people of God as Moses was in Israel (17:10). Moses had revealed the Lord to the people, but Jesus had manifested His name fully (17:6). Because of the great love each had for their people, both wanted them to enjoy intimacy with God (17:21–24) and to this end had passed God's Word on to them (17:14).

We glimpse here the type of prayer that prevails with God. It comes from the surrendered heart of one who confidently but humbly trusts God to keep His promises (2 Samuel 7:25; Romans 4:20). Using human language the authors tell us that the Lord relented and did not bring about the threatened disaster (v.14). We see the necessity of a mediator in God's redemptive plan; but for such a mediator our sinfulness would draw down His judgement on us (cf. James 1:17).

Moses the Judge (32:15–30)

During his descent of the mountain Moses found the faithful Joshua, who had waited patiently for him all this time – what a contrast to the infidelity and impatience of the people! Joshua was to become a worthy successor to Moses. Moses carried the two Tables of the Testimony in his hands; the work of God – God's own handwriting! (vv.15,16). It is emphasized here that the Law was God's revelation, not the work of man. As they approached the camp the uproar reached them. Joshua thought it was the sound of battle, but Moses knew otherwise (vv.17–18). As the sight of the people, the orgiastic dancing and revelry before the golden calf, came into their view, Moses realized why God had been angry, for he felt that blazing anger within himself now. He threw the Tables of Stone towards the people and broke them at the foot of the mountain, a powerful gesture declaring the Covenant between the Lord and the people formally broken (v.19). This meant that the people, knowingly, had brought down the consequences on themselves. Suddenly the revelry was changed into silent horror. Their loving redeemer, Moses, had turned judge! For us too Jesus will be our gentle, loving saviour or judge depending on whether we acknowledge our sins and are converted, or whether we force Him by our obduracy to judge us (Matthew 23:13–36). They had entered the Covenant open-eyed: before it was solemnly ratified they had several opportunities to back down, but no! They declared, 'All that the Lord said, we will do' (cf. 19:3–8, 25, 20:1–21, 24:3–4, 7–8). Now they stood back in silence as Moses showed them the consequences of their actions.

He seized the calf and burnt it to powder – the secret of how to do this was known to the Egyptians – thus reducing this so-called god to the 'nothing' it really was. It was plain to all that this 'calf' had no power before the blazing anger of Moses, let alone before the Lord! Next followed the trial by ordeal, to separate the innocent from the guilty – a common custom in the ancient world – where Moses scattered the gold dust on the water supply and made the people drink it (v.20) (cf. Numbers 5:11–31). He then turned to upbraid Aaron for his part in the affair, just as God turned to Adam first after the Fall. As Adam blamed Eve for his sin so here Aaron blamed the people (vv.21–24), but neither here, nor later (Numbers 12:1–16) when he and Miriam rebelled against Moses, was Aaron punished. In the latter incident Miriam was the only one of the three concerned who was not the anointed one of the Lord, so she bore Aaron's guilt! It seems that even God will not touch His anointed ones! (cf. 1 Chronicles 16:22; Psalm 105:15). What a salutary lesson in reverence to God's consecrated priests, whether they deserve it by the quality of their lives or not. Since they are the Lord's anointed ones, He recognizes that fact – so must we.

The people had broken loose from law and order, and only a salutary punishment would restore the camp to right relationship with God and each other (v.25). When he challenged the people to declare themselves for God or not, only the Tribe of Levi rallied to him, indicating the depth of the problem. As a test of the Levites' sincerity and determination to serve God at any cost to themselves, Moses ordered them to execute the guilty – even if they were members of their own family. They obeyed, and three thousand people died that day, for the wages of sin is death! The feasting of the morning led to mourning by evening. Such is sin, which always leaves a trail of disaster in its wake. The fact that neither Moses nor the Levites were resisted, shows that Moses was the visible sign of the Lord's presence among them and that they recognized God's Word through him (vv.27–28). The zeal of the Levites for the Lord was seen as a sign that they were the right choice for the priesthood – a priest without zeal for the father's glory is a contradiction (v.29; cf. Numbers 25:7–13; Deuteronomy 33:8–11; John 2:17).

This picture of Moses as judge foreshadows the second

coming of Jesus, when He will descend from the heavenly sanctuary to judge His people by the two-fold law of love (Matthew 22:37–40; 25:31–46). He is now 'absent' from us in His ascension glory, prefigured by Moses in God's presence on the Mount. Like Moses He is aware of all that happens in His Church: 'I know all about you' (Revelation chapters 2 and 3), and the time for reaping what we have sown will surely come, as it did for Israel (Genesis 6:7–8; 2 Thessalonians 1:8–10).

The idolatry, with all its sensuality, represents the 'flesh' and its power to pull us down if not kept in its place by self-control. The zeal of the Levites points to the Spirit in us overcoming the flesh by 'crucifying it' so that God can reign among us (Genesis 5:24). The weapons of *our* warfare are not carnal but spiritual (2 Corinthians 10:4), and the sword in our hand is not the sword of destruction but the sword of the Spirit (the scriptures), through which we are guided by God to keep the flesh in its place, lest it rebel (Ephesians 6:17). Jesus, too, will reward those who overcome, just as Moses did the Israelites. The Levites were rewarded with the priesthood, but we will be given the Tree of Life in Paradise (Revelation 2:7). We will have nothing to fear from hell (Revelation 2:11); we will be given a hidden manna and a new name (Revelation 2:17), plus authority over the pagans (Revelation 2:25), while becoming pillars in the heavenly sanctuary with the name of God, of the heavenly city and the Lamb inscribed on us (Revelation 3:12). Finally we will be allowed to share the throne of the Lamb! (Revelation 3:21). What an incentive to put away idols and crucify the flesh for only thus will the Kingdom of God reign in us!

The following day Moses confronted the people who, as yet, have shown no sign of repentance. They were shocked and grieved over their punishment, but repentance is a change of heart. Since this had not occurred, Moses confronted them with their sin and their need for atonement (v.30). Will they ask their mediator to atone for them? Will they humbly beg him to intercede for them?

No! They stand in silence as Moses goes back to the Lord. It is frightening to observe the stubborn refusal of sinners to repent as they resist grace after grace, almost forcing God to use the heavy hand on them. Even then they may use the punishment as an excuse to walk away, saying that He is a vengeful God! Poor God! All He wants is a loving people in union with Him and each other, but it seems almost impossible to achieve! (v.30).

Moses the Intercessor (32:31–33:7)

Moses returned to the Lord because he was pre-eminently a man of prayer. In every decision and crisis he is found on his knees before God, seeking to know God's will in order to obey it. He foreshadows Jesus, the man of prayer, who is portrayed in the gospels as seeking to know the Father's will on all occasions (cf. Mark 1:35; Luke 2:49f, chapter 4, etc.). Moses, grieved in heart over the people, made a national confession to God (v.31), while his great love for the people urged him to offer himself as substitute for their sin (v.32). How closely he resembles Jesus now, the one who in fact offered Himself as the sacrifice that takes away our sins. Love was the motivation in both cases, but as it was not yet the time for Calvary God replied that the guilty should die for their sin, not the innocent (v.33); hence the death penalty was imposed (v.35).

Order to Depart (33:1–6)

God now ordered Moses to break camp and depart from Sinai. The people had been long enough around this mountain and they needed the hazards of the journey to keep them out of mischief and to keep them seeking God (v.34; cf. Deuteronomy 1:6). There was just one problem – a major one: the Lord refused to go with them! He would give them a guardian angel instead who would guide them all the way (32:34, 33:2). It was good news that they could proceed to the Promised Land – but without the Lord?

Without God it would be just like any other land! It was the Lord who would make it flow with milk and honey and drive out the inhabitants for them. He was their joy and their life, without Him all was death. He refused to go with them because His holiness and their sinfulness were incompatible, so He ordered them to take off their ornaments as a sign of mourning (vv.2–5). On hearing this awful news the people obeyed and went into mourning – the first hopeful sign of repentance. What a tragedy it is when God's people are indifferent to whether He is present with them or not. This is the terrible malaise in the Church today (Revelation 3:15). At least Israel knew it was a tragedy to lose God's presence, and she began to humble herself before Him by this act of obedience (cf. 1 Corinthians 4:18–21; 2 Corinthians 7:8–9).

Since the sanctuary was not yet built Moses removed the Tent of Meeting, placing it outside the camp to show them that the Lord was no longer in their midst. He was outside, bearing the shame of the people (v.7; Hebrews 13:14), but He was still willing to receive anyone who would agree to go outside the camp to meet Him. We see here again that He tempered judgement with mercy, for the way was still open for those who wanted to seek Him. They were chastened, not cut off. The sad thing was that from this time onward His glory would be hidden from them in the sanctuary and would be revealed to very few (cf. Numbers 12:7–80; Deuteronomy 34:10; 1 Kings 19:11f). They had forfeited the privileged glory of Sinai and they must proceed on their journey with the weight of their sinfulness heavy upon them.

Moses the Friend of God (33:8–23)

The stature of Moses, the man of God, stands out in bold relief against the background of this sinful nation. His humility and obedience are constant, while his fiery love of God and neighbour is seen in his selfless service to both. We will now glimpse some of the intimacy this great man enjoyed with God – all the more bright against the dark background of sin. The contrast will show us what the people lost by rebellion and what we can gain by fidelity to God's will.

Whenever Moses went out to the Tent to meet God the people would stand at the door of their tents in silent reverence. The Pillar of Cloud would descend and station itself at the entrance to the Tent, and there the Lord would speak to Moses while the people bowed low in worship at a distance. The Lord spoke to Moses as a man speaks to his friend. Afterwards Moses would return to his tent, leaving the faithful Joshua in God's presence (vv.8–11). Now God's promise to Moses in Exodus 19:9 has come true: 'I am coming to you in a dense cloud so that the people may hear when I speak to you and may trust you always.' Moses had undisputed leadership and the trust of the nation now; but it had been gained at great cost to himself and his people. This is a vital point, for the redemptive process could not be completed if the people rejected the divinely appointed Saviour (cf. John 6:67, 14:1, 17:3), for God was, in and through Moses, reconciling Israel to Himself just as He did for all mankind through Jesus (2 Corinthians 5:19). Moses did not see God face to face (33:20). The authors of Exodus want to tell us that God revealed Himself to Moses with greater clarity and evidence of divine light than He did to any of the other prophets, and his closeness to God foreshadowed the intimate union of Jesus with the Father (John 14:9–10, 10–29).

An interesting point regarding Joshua: since his appointment as army commander (Exodus 17) he was being prepared to take over the leadership from Moses. One of the qualifications needed was intimacy with God; we have seen him waiting for forty days on the Mount for Moses to return. Now he kept vigil at the Tent of Meeting. It was training in prayer, in obedience and selflessness. The forty years of Israel wandering in the wilderness was his training ground, just as it had been for Moses previously.

219

At the end Joshua was to know God sufficiently well to be able to lead the people to the Promised Land and to discern God's will for them just as Moses did. Apprenticeship to a master was good training indeed.

Moses used his privileged intimacy to prevail on the Lord to come back and lead Israel again. He did not know who their newly appointed companion was (32:34), and yet the Lord had said that Moses found favour with Him (v.12). He then asked the Lord to reveal Himself more deeply so that he could understand His ways more clearly and still find favour with Him (v.13). His request was like this: 'Let me understand you, so that I can relate to you better, then perhaps I can handle this crisis, but if this is the end of all negotiation we are finished.' A crisis reveals new depths in the persons involved. Here Moses expressed the deepest need in all of us – to know how to get around the heart of our Father – God (cf. Psalm 25:4, 16:11, 27:11, etc.). The Lord's reply seems strange: 'My presence will go with you and I will give you rest', because in 34:9 Moses is still pleading with the Lord to come with them. The Companion Bible suggests that it may be a question: 'Shall my presence go with you and shall I give you rest – after all the rejection and apostasy?' Moses' reply now makes sense: 'If you are not coming with us, don't ask us to depart from here!' The distinguishing mark of this nation of Israel was the Lord Himself! Without Him they were nothing and Moses knew this, as did their enemies (v.16; cf. 1 Samuel 4:4–8). The Lord granted his request because of His friendship with Moses (v.17). It is lovely to see that Moses could not bear to depart from Sinai, if the Lord, the treasure of his heart, was left behind.

Emboldened by his success, Moses requested that God should show him His glory (v.18). The Lord's reply was to show him His splendour (JB), goodness (RSV), beauty (NAB) instead – but the full vision of God, to see Him face to face, is reserved for heaven (cf. 1 Timothy 6:16). Here Moses expressed the longing for greater intimacy of all souls who know God – their aching need to 'see' Him – but the more He reveals Himself the greater is their need for 'more' of Him, until death tears the veil away and we see Him face to face, to our ecstatic joy and eternal delight. God responded partially to Moses' request here – but fully on Mount Nebo some years later (cf. Deuteronomy 34). Even for the partial revelation Moses needed to be protected by the cleft in the rock and God's hand in order to survive it (vv. 19–23).

It was then that God fulfilled the request Moses had made at the burning bush (Exodus 3). All He revealed to Moses then was that He was the great 'I AM', but now, as His glory passed by, God proclaimed who He was in seven-fold perfection: He is a God of Mercy (tenderness) and compassion (graciousness), slow to anger (patient), abounding in loving-kindness and fidelity, keeping his steadfast love for thousands, forgiving faults, transgression and sin, but also the God who will let nothing go unchecked, visiting the father's fault on the sons and grandsons to the third and fourth generation (34:6–7; cf. Numbers 16:32; Joshua 7:24–25; Matthew 27:25). Before this blinding revelation Moses bowed to the ground in worship, realizing that God *had* shown him His ways and how to relate to Him! (Exodus 33:13). The people *needed* a merciful God who would be understanding of their faults and remain faithful to them nevertheless; the Lord was the right god for this people! What joy! Of course, as a good parent, He would have to chastise them. The only 'glory' that a sinner could endure would be the loving-kindness of God our saviour (cf. Titus 3:4–7). Now that Moses knew how to deal with God, he begged Him to travel with the people, and even to adopt them as His heritage, which He did (34:9); (cf. Psalm 33:13, 94:14; Ephesians 1:8). We can now see why God gave them the Tabernacle and its worship, as He intended dealing with them in Mercy.

For us Jesus is both the Rock and the Mercy of God to sinners. All his ministry demonstrated His loving-kindness to those willing to admit their sin. Mercy is that attribute of God revealed to those who are unable to keep His Law

– surely a revelation of splendour and beauty! It means love given to the undeserving, and that quality of love which 'bends over backwards' to reach the other. It is also the giving beyond the ability to recall 'how much' – such is the steadfast love of God. We see yet again in the incident of the golden calf that God brings good out of evil and lets the sin of man occasion a deeper revelation of Himself.

These seven qualities of God explain all of God's dealings with Israel subsequently; *Mercy* 2 Samuel 24:14; 1 Kings 3:6, 8:23; Jeremiah 3:12; Isaiah 54:7; Jeremiah 42:12; Psalm 86:15, etc.; *Patience* Nehemiah 9:18; Matthew 23:37; *Loving-kindness* Psalm 36:7, 48:9, 63:7; *Faithfulness* Psalm 78:35–38; *Forgiveness* Jeremiah 31:34, etc.

Transfiguration of Moses (Chapter 34)

The Lord called Moses up the mountain again. He was to bring two new tables of stone so that God could inscribe the the Ten Living Words again and re-establish His covenant with Israel (vv.1–2). Before ascending the mountain at dawn the following day Moses left strict orders regarding the distance to be kept by the people (vv.3–5). The Cloud of God's presence descended, and in wondrous grace the Lord offered not only to renew the Covenant but to work more wonders for Israel than for any other nation on earth! (v.10). During another forty-day period God discussed the Covenant with Moses, who was to write it down under His inspiration (v.27). Henceforth the scriptures would come to us through the mediation of men. When Jesus came He released God's Law from the accretions of the centuries; He showed the spirit behind the letter, and revealed God's original intention in giving it. He also raised the standard to the level of the Spirit (cf. Matthew 5–7), writing the Law on our hearts where the Holy Spirit would enable us to live it.

On his descent from the Mount Moses found the people

reconciled to God and at peace. There was no disorder in the camp this time. He held the two new Tables of Stone, and did not realize that his face radiated the glory of God, so that the people were afraid to approach him. He called Aaron and the leaders to him and gradually the people came too (v.29–32). The glory on Moses' face touched their hearts, and they knew that *they* could not stand in the August Presence Moses had tolerated for so long. The authors of Exodus place this incident in the text just before the building of the Tabernacle, when the Shekinah Glory would come to dwell with them. The people caught a glimpse of that glory in Moses' face.

The transfiguration of Moses points to the transfiguration of Jesus on Mount Tabor. The glory on Moses' face illustrates what we said of the people in the worship of the golden calf, namely that we become like unto that which we worship. The psalmist said, 'Every face turned to *Him* grows brighter and is never ashamed' (Psalm 34:5). The face and behaviour of Moses tells us who his God was, just as the sinful behaviour of the people told theirs. Nevertheless the glory of Moses was that of a creature reflecting the glory of God, whereas Jesus *is* the glory of God, hidden in the Incarnation but revealed momentarily on Tabor: 'He is the radiant light of God's glory and the perfect copy of His nature . . .' (Hebrews 1:3).

St Paul interprets this passage in 2 Corinthians 3:6–18. There he calls the Sinaitic Law a law which brought death, as illustrated in the three thousand deaths after the worship of the golden calf, whereas the New Covenant was written in the Spirit and administers eternal life (2 Corinthians 3–6). The splendour of the revelation to Moses cannot be compared to that of Jesus which brought justification, instead of the Mosaic law which showed up sin and therefore brought condemnation (2 Corinthians 3:7–11). The Jewish people today cannot behold, as we do, the glory of God in the face of Christ, because there is a veil over their minds, which Christ alone can remove, and will remove when they turn to Him (2 Corinthians 3:12–17). In the meantime we Christians are to contemplate Christ in prayer, reflect Him in our daily lives, and be gradually transformed into His image – all of which is the work of the Holy Spirit in us (2 Corinthians 3:18, 4:6).

To the Promised Land (40:36–38)

Now that the Lord had revealed the attributes of His character needed to deal with sinners, and had given them the Tabernacle and a system of worship that would keep the people in relationship with Him, they could continue their journey to the Promised Land. They had learned to their cost not to go ahead of the Lord or His servant Moses in decision-making. Instead they were to follow the leadership of Moses who in turn, followed the Lord. Henceforth at each stage of the journey, whenever the Cloud rose from the Tabernacle, Israel would resume her march, but if the Cloud rested on the Tabernacle she waited (40:36–37). The Lord, her glory, was in her midst and she would not risk losing Him again. He knew the way to the Promised Land, she did not, so He carved a way for her through that trackless wasteland until she reached home, and rest, in the land of promise (Book of Joshua).

I am the Way . . . I am the Light of the world; he who follows me will not be walking in the dark; he will have the light of life.

(John 7:12, 14:6)

Jesus has carved the way for us all, the way back to the Father, to home . . . to Heaven.